SIMONE SHIVON

MAJESTIC RAINBOW LOVE

YOUR SACRED INITIATORY
TO RETURN AS THE DIVINE CHILD

MAJESTIC RAINBOW LOVE

YOUR SACRED INITIATORY
TO RETURN AS THE DIVINE CHILD

BY SIMONE SHIVON

MAJESTIC RAINBOW PUBLISHING | UNITED STATES

Majestic Rainbow Publishing

Portland, Oregon,
United States

All information contained within this book is for general information
and spiritual purposes. Portions of this book are works of nonfiction.
Certain names and identifying characteristics have been changed.

ISBN Paperback# – 979-8-9861916-0-7

ISBN Hardback# – 979-8-9861916-1-4

ISBN Electronic# – 979-8-9861916-2-1

Illustrations by Simone Shivon on pages XV, 3, 23, 26, 75-76, 80, 83,
90, 92, 95, 98, 100, 115, 102-115, 153, 204, 206-219, 228, 267, 277
Illustrations by Milla Bioni Guerra, book cover and on page 79.
Illustrations by Jo Beth Young on pages 2, 22, 74, 266
Illustrations by Li Wei on pages IV and 277

鶴夢願圓

一切皆緣　一切皆空

一切皆色　一切源緣愛

鶴夢願圓

hè mèng yuàn yuan

一切皆缘，

yī qiè jiē yuan,

一切皆空，

yī qiè jiē kōng

一切皆色，

yī qiè jiē sè

一切源缘爱。

yī qiè yuán yuán ài

† 梓瑪・瑞安 †

TRANSLATION:
THE TRANSCENDENTAL DREAM

Everything is a touch through serendipity,

Everything is created from nothingness,

Everything is filled with colors,

Everything is rooted in love.

† SIMONE SHIVON †

TABLE OF CONTENTS

FOREWORD

When I first read *Majestic Rainbow Love*, I felt privileged to get insight into a new and beautiful philosophy that felt both familiar and timeless, yet progressive and advanced. I was struck by the energy I felt shifting within me, and by the subtle—yet profound—momentum of each movement in the book.

Many people have written about healing and the realm of the inner child, but Simone Shivon's debut book is my first experience of reading and fully understanding the archetype of the cosmic child: which to me is the inner child healed, the inner child ascended, and the union of the divine masculine and feminine self. By healing and activating the light body in this way, Simone Shivon shows us how "oneness" can be experienced and born within at an energetic level, which in turn will manifest in our individual and collective lives. It is the next step. This is one of the many reasons you are about to experience an extraordinary reconnection within as you read the following pages.

These children's stories for adults transmit a magical energy intricately and cleverly woven through repetitions of our true self, our natural state and of true self enquiry that could be likened to the power of mantra. This book is pure transmission that transcends the thinking mind and speaks directly to the heart and subconscious mind, leaving you at the next turn on the spiral of your evolution. You will read it again and again—and each time, you will absorb and embody more wisdom.

Simone Shivon's words feel beyond time and space and are a direct path to the oneness and freedom at the core of one's true nature. We are after all, children of the Universe. This book goes straight to the heart of what that means and how to access it. It is not an airy-fairy notion; it is powerful and unique to anything I have read before—and is all the more special for it.

As someone who has assisted others to heal from trauma and to re-connect to their true, wild self, this book is a valuable resource. *Majestic Rainbow Love* is not simply a book, it is an *experience*. Allow yourself to absorb its musical, mystical flow—you will be transformed.

JO BETH YOUNG

Wisdom Teacher, Founder of Wildness Rising
Award Winning Recording Artist

PREFACE

Most of us are aware that within us there lives the four divine aspects referred to as the "Inner Child," "Cosmic Child," "Divine Masculine," and "Divine Feminine," but what has been less commonly discussed is the Divine Child. In this new era humanity has just entered, the Divine Child is being called forth for deeper understanding and healing, to assist our re-embodiment and return to life as the Divine Child.

The Divine Child is our original innocent state of being, the way we were divinely created to be at the dawn of time. This child represents the awakening of our diamond light body, where we are in union with all aspects of self—a state of enlightenment. Our re-embodiment as the Divine Child can be comprehended as the awakening and the union of our four divine aspects—the "Inner Child" "Cosmic Child," "Divine Masculine" and "Divine Feminine." This is done through constant refining our inner balance, to bring all aspects of ourselves together as one. Our inner balance is not a fixed point; it is unique within each one of us, and shifts with our inner movement through time and life constantly. Therefore, our re-embodiment requires our devotion to love in Divine Union throughout our lives.

On a soul level, our re-embodiment represents the reclamation of our sovereignty as a divine creation. In this state of being, we expand our love from self-love to love toward our family, our community, our country, and our world just the way it is, without bypassing any of them. As we stand as the Divine Child, we experience our unique gifts, healing powers, innate wisdom, and divine miracles. Thus, we attain our self-realizations through life. As the Divine Child, we can now Co-create United Eternal Sanctuary (CUES) on earth. As part of the divine tapestry, we fulfill the prophecy of heaven on earth as humanity.

CUES—"Co-create United Eternal Sanctuary" is the eternal vision of the divine council—where its mission is to assist us human beings to live in love and unity with all of creations. This vision reflects the dream behind the Divine's creation of the earth at the dawn of time—heaven on earth.

Majestic Rainbow Love was first unveiled to me from the divine in 2012, subtly as an energetic divine gateway. It is created as part of the eternal vision—CUES, to assist humanity to return to our original innocent state of being—the Divine Child. In 2014, I was ordained and initiated by the divine council to be The Guardian of the Majestic Rainbow Love, and to be The Keeper of The Eternal Flame—the divine flame of love and unity. Even though understanding what it truly means to be The Guardian and The Keeper will take me a lifetime in communion, part of my sacred vocation is to translate for humanity (from its original form of energy vibration) the divine wisdom of Majestic Rainbow Love, to assist others return to the state of the Divine Child. Additionally, I am granted the responsibility of holding The Eternal Flame—a vibrational healing light, as an anchor on Earth. Through my communion over the last decade, I have translated different sections of its wisdom into cipher oracle decks and alchemical potions.

In 2019, I was divinely called to bring through the macro-view of Majestic Rainbow Love to humanity. I have written its wisdom into a total of 29 ciphers, consisting of 5,684 divine codes. These 29 ciphers became the original text of this book, called *Majestic Rainbow Love Ciphers*. Its purpose is to provide humanity with a macro-view of how we can navigate on this non-linear spiritual pilgrimage and return as the Divine Child. In 2021, I was divinely guided to translate these ciphers into modern human language as an energetic extension of this gateway for humanity. Thus these translations have lead to the birth of this book.

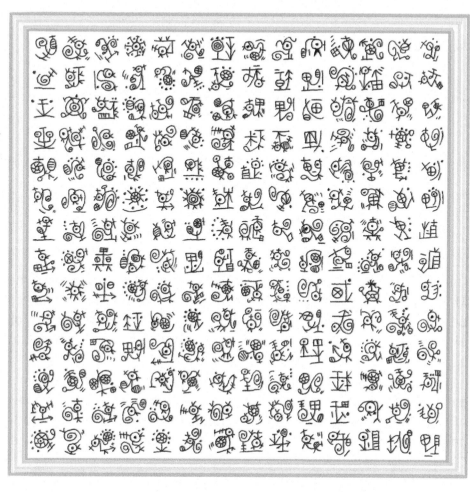

"The Majestic Rainbow Love Cipher: No.0 — I AM I"

INTRODUCTION

This book—*Majestic Rainbow Love*—is an energetic extension of the Majestic Rainbow Love gateway, written as a sacred initiation and embedded with energy transmissions. It aims to provide you with an overall experience of the gateway and an understanding of its philosophy to assist your return as the Divine Child.

This sacred initiation is constructed of four movements as its core structure, representing the four rites of passage of the gateway. The four rites of passage reactivate the four strands of your diamond light body, and represent the four divine aspects—the Divine Masculine, the Inner Child, the Divine Feminine, and the Cosmic Child. When your illusion of separation in duality dissolves, you experience Divine Union—the wholeness of your divinity. This sets the ground and marks the beginning of your union with all creations, where you reclaim your throne to Co-create United Eternal Sanctuary (CUES).

�֍

Here are the missions of the four rites of passage:
1. The First Rite of Passage is an initiation into your remembrance of your divinity,

2. The Second Rite of Passage is an initiation into your reconnection with your spirit,
3. The Third Rite of Passage is an initiation into your rebirth as the Divine Child, and
4. The Fourth Rite of Passage is an initiation into your re-embodiment as the Divine Child.

Majestic Rainbow Love's sacred scroll—The Š—is the philosophy of the gateway. It is also a nonlinear healing system which serves as a way of sacred living. It provides you a perspective on how Divine Love can be experienced in duality on Earth, within and without. The Š consists of four passages:

✦ The Š Doctrine,
✦ The Š Bell,
✦ The Š Matrix, and
✦ The Š Testimony.

This is the healing system that enables you to reunite with your four divine aspects as one. Ultimately, this brings you to wholeness—you reclaim your divine power, and navigate your sacred pilgrimage in life through your conscious intuitive logic and innate wisdom.

This initiation is designed in a bespoke format with the flair of a children's story book, and it conveys through the ancient way of spiritual initiations. Our souls absorb information effectively through our hearts, in the intangible form of vibrational energy. Therefore, all words, ciphers, and graphics here are embedded with energy transmissions. They are incorporated to transform your soul through your heart and beyond your mind. When your soul transforms, your mind and your way of living follows. Thus, the Divine Child within you reawakens from The Void of nothingness, and your life transforms.

Living in the Š way enables you to hold unconditional love toward all of creations, and to love eternally as a light being. By living this way, your life (including the wisdom you have attained, the divine creations you have birthed, and the lives have you touched, etc.) becomes a selfless service to humanity. Hence, you witness the majesty of the divine and your existence.

To begin to experience yourself as the Divine Child, you must first open your heart to believe and trust this sacred initiation. This initiation often feels like there is no beginning and no end, as if you are walking in spirals within The Void of nothingness. This initiation is to provide you with a taste of what eternity feels like in a body. Hence, it shows you where healings are needed so you can reach immortality. Your feelings and your ability to walk in infinite spirals are keys to experience heaven on earth in duality.

Due to the nature of this initiation, strong emotions, questions, or even physical discomforts are designed to be stirred up, so they can be healed. It is when you begin to feel and to question, you can begin to heal and dissolve your blockages. As you read, it is crucial that you take notes of your emotions and questions when they arise. These are personalized hints that show you where healings are needed. All these can be healed and dissolved through you living by "The Š".

Since this book is a living transmission, it is not uncommon that your mind will drift away as you expand your consciousness and your light body. Thus, it is vital that you allow yourself to rest whenever you feel any discomfort or you find yourself drifting off when reading this book. This way, you will allow deeper transmissions to anchor and integrate within your being.

Potential unpleasant emotions
- ♥ Numbness—As you release numbness, you know your soul.
- ♥ Depression—As you release depression, you see love from within.
- ♥ Abandonment—As you release abandonment, you hear the divine.
- ♥ Anger—As you release anger, you smell sweetness in life.
- ♥ Confusion—As you release confusion, you taste your Divine Union.
- ♥ Hesitancy—As you release hesitancy, you feel your passion.
- ♥ Anxiety—As you release anxiety, you touch sacred harmony.

Potential physical discomfort
- ♥ Flu symptoms—As you release flu symptoms, you rebalance your immunity.
- ♥ Diarrhea—As you release diarrhea, you rebalance your digestion.
- ♥ Headache—As you release headache, you rebalance your five elements.
- ♥ Muscle spasm—As you release muscle spasm, you rebalance your chi.
- ♥ Nausea—As you release nausea, you rebalance your blood.
- ♥ Night sweats—As you release night sweats, you rebalance your yin–yang balance.
- ♥ Fatigue—As you release fatigue, you rebalance whole-being.

Here are the four keys to walking through the initiation.
- ✦ Be present.
- ✦ Be devoted.
- ✦ Be accepting.
- ✦ Be honest.

The end of your initiation—going through the four rites of passage, marks the beginning of your return to life as the Divine Child. You then begin to Co-create United Eternal Sanctuary (CUES) side by side with other ascended beings. Hence, your life is transformed; You experience Divine Love and sacred harmony within and without. Moreover, our humanity and the earth will transform naturally because of your re-embodiment.

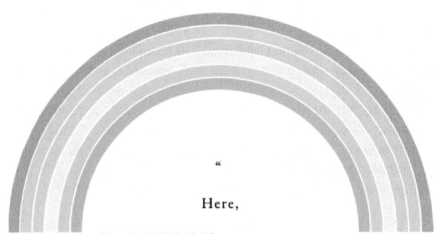

"

Here,

You REMEMBER your true nature,

You RECONNECT with your soul.

You CREATE from your heart,

You LIVE out your dream,

As The Divine Child.

Embody

Who

You

Are

Now

!

"

† Simone Shivon †

Is this book a story?
Is this book not a story?
"This is Love."

Is this book an initiation?
Is this book not an initiation?
"This is Love."

Is this book a philosophy?
Is this book not a philosophy?
"This is Love."

Is this book a pilgrimage?
Is this book not a pilgrimage?
"This is Love."

Is this ... ?
"This is Love."

Is this ... ?
"This is Love."

Is this ... ?
"This is Love."

Why? What? Where? Who? When? W ... ? W ... ? W ... ? W ... ?
"All is Loved."

My beloved children, leave your questions here.

From nothingness, you begin your sacred initiation now.

Here ... You begin your sacred initiation.
    Now ... You drop your mind into your heart.
        You enter the gateway of Majestic Rainbow Love.

    Breathe in deeply and repeat after me ...

Š

Šhhhh ...
Šhhhh ...
Šhhhh ...
Šhhhh ...

Breathe in deeply and repeat after me ...

Š

Šhhhh ...
Šhhhh ...
Šhhhh ...
Šhhhh ...

Breathe in deeply and Repeat after me ...

Š

Šhhhh ...
Šhhhh ...
Šhhhh ...
Šhhhh ...

Breathe in deeply and repeat after me ...

Š

Šhhhh ...
Šhhhh ...
Šhhhh ...
Šhhhh ...

FIRST Š MOVEMENT

THE REMEMBRANCE THROUGH
EXPLORATIONS

22	9	24	77	24	9	22
4	3	8	11	8	3	4
12	66	7	1	7	66	12
6	11	2	?	2	11	6
12	66	7	1	7	66	12
4	3	8	11	8	3	4
22	9	24	77	24	9	22

"The Explorations"

*Place your left hand on the square to begin your First Rite of Passage. Allow the energy to activate your light body.

WHO AM I?
Is This a Question?
Is This Not a Question?

MA'S RAINBOW FAM.

Under tonight's Blood Moon, scarlet and golden maple leaves blow in the autumn wind. Breathing in the loamy earthy air, Grandma MA clutches her seven love letters to her heart. Quietly, eyes filled with tears of gratitude, she prays and sends love into each letter. "Once upon a time, I dreamed that one day I would live in a rainbow world of love and unity." She closes her eyes.

Grandma MA's mind wanders back to that sacred day: The seventh of July. Flashes of memories arise. She soliloquizes:

Long, long ago ... one summer night, I was sleeping in my cozy house beside the ocean. Suddenly, lightning struck through the center of my body! I woke up. But I couldn't open my eyes or move my body. I couldn't think, feel, or see. My body was frozen. I was shocked. When I could, I opened my eyes and realized I was in a world where everything emanated a rainbow hue. With curiosity, I began my exploration of this land. During this pilgrimage, forty-nine of my fellows showed up. Even though it took me a long while, I remembered our eternal connections through our touches of love and we were re-united in the end.

No words can describe the majesty of my expedition: it was beyond magical. There I had the chance to explore my soul, experience my sacred gifts, experiment with cosmic creations, and expedite my divine embodiment.

Before I was transported back into this reality, I was ordained as The Guardian of this divine gateway—Majestic Rainbow Love. And I was appointed as The Keeper of The Eternal Flame. Honestly, I was clueless about what it meant to be a guardian and a keeper. I did ask my fellows, but all they did was wrap their love around me with a smile. I was left in the state of "I Don't Know." All they did was to encourage me to say, "Yes, I DO." I wonder if anyone is capable of rejecting Divine Love? Soaking in their love, my heart melted. Eventually, I said "YES." Now, I am grateful that I let go of the need to compartmentalize everything. I allowed myself to surrender into the unknown. In the end, Melchizedek cloaked me with the Š Divine Diamond—a diamond with infinite facets filled with colors. Under this cloak, I was glowing within and without, "I know I AM Love." I received it with deep gratitude. Melchizedek pronounced. "Now, only those whose heart can see will see you. Under the divine order, you shall become ... ."

Being Transported back to my room, I fell on my knees. I looked out the window—was I dreaming? Or am I dreaming now? I saw the same ocean, its endless waves singing. The sun was shining, the birds were soaring, my heart was beating. I wondered—Who? Who Am I? I Don't Know, I Don't Know, I Don't Know ...

In this mist of the unknown, every morning for seven consecutive days, a swaddled infant was placed in a basket at my front door. Each child was wrapped in a blanket of a different color with their name written in a love note, which said—"Please Guide The Child Home."

"Grandma MA! Where Are YOU AGAIN? Grandma MAaaa ..." The children scream.

"I AM Coming!" Grandma MA scribbles their names on the front of the letter swiftly with the dragon blood ink, and seals each letter with love: Sofia, Celeste, Amira, Godfrey, Andrea, Celsa, Jeff.

Seven years fly by. All the children have grown up with their own essence, flourishing with their unique sacred healing abilities. Yet, they hold these traits in common: their hearts are filled with pure Divine Love, wisdom, and power, and their enormous, innocent eyes that see deep into the souls of others.

LOVE LETTERS FROM MA

MA's Letter to Sofia

Dear Sofia,

Dancing around,
Sprinkling roses wherever you go.
Empowered like the Lotus-Rose, you now glow.

You; the Mother, the Goddess in our rainbow family.
With your pure, innocent heart at the core of your spirituality.
You brought infinite love with you into our duality.
We are forever a family.
Happily, Gracefully, Unshakably
We are forever MA's Rainbow Fam.

I will never forget the first day you arrived,
Wrapped in a purple blanket with your big, sparkling eyes;
Always filled with Divine Love and so wise.
Thank you for coming into my life.
Our love knot is forever tied.
You are my pride.

MA.
7/7/∞

MA's Letter to Celeste

Dear Celeste,

Whirling around,
Sprinkling mushrooms wherever you go.
Magical like the moon, you now glow.

You, the Fairy, the Mystic in our rainbow family.
With your pure, innocent heart at the core of your spirituality.
You brought infinite healing with you into our duality.
We are forever a family.
Happily, Gracefully, Unshakably.
We are forever MA's Rainbow Fam.

I will never forget the first day you arrived,
Wrapped in a blue blanket with your big, sparkling eyes;
Always filled with Divine Love and so enchanted.
Thank you for coming into my life.
Our love knot is forever tied.
You are my pride.

MA.
7/7/∞

MA's Letter to Amira

Dear Amira,

Sitting around,
Sprinkling spices wherever you go.
Glorious like a star, you now glow.

You, the Yogi, the Seeress in our rainbow family.
With your pure, innocent heart at the core of your spirituality.
You brought infinite wisdom with you into our duality.
We are forever a family.
Happily, Gracefully, Unshakably.
We are forever MA's Rainbow Fam.

I will never forget the first day you arrived,
Wrapped in a green blanket with your big, sparkling eyes;
Always filled with Divine Love and so insightful.
Thank you for coming into my life.
Our love knot is forever tied.
You are my pride.

MA.
7/7/∞

MA's Letter to Godfrey

Dear Godfrey,

Parading around,
Sprinkling frankincense wherever you go.
Sturdy like gold, you now glow.

You, the Minister, the Alchemist in our rainbow family.
With your pure, innocent heart at the core of your spirituality.
You brought infinite will with you into our duality.
We are forever a family.
Happily, Gracefully, Unshakably.
We are forever MA's Rainbow Fam.

I will never forget the first day you arrived,
Wrapped in a yellow blanket with your big, sparkling eyes;
Always filled with Divine Love and so powerful.
Thank you for coming into my life.
Our love knot is forever tied.
You are my pride.

MA.
7/7/∞

MA's Letter to Andrea

Dear Andrea,

Ambling around,
Sprinkling pine cones wherever you go.
Blaze like the sun. You now glow.

You, the Musician, the Herbalist in our rainbow family.
With your pure innocent heart at the core of your spirituality.
You brought infinite humility with you into our duality.
We are forever a family.
Happily, Gracefully, Unshakably.
We are forever MA's Rainbow Fam.

I will never forget the first day you arrived,
Wrapped in an orange blanket with your big, sparkling eyes;
Always filled with Divine Love and so generous.
Thank you for coming into my life.
Our love knot is forever tied.
You are my pride.

MA.
7/7/∞

MA's Letter to Celsa

Dear Celsa,

Swirling around,
Sprinkling olives wherever you go.
Innocent like a pearl, you now glow.

You, the Artist, the Enchantress in our rainbow family.
With your pure, innocent heart at the core of your spirituality.
You brought infinite manifestations with you into our duality.
We are forever a family.
Happily, Gracefully, Unshakably.
We are forever MA's Rainbow Fam.

I will never forget the first day you arrived,
Wrapped in a pink blanket with your big, sparkling eyes;
Always filled with Divine Love and so graceful.
Thank you for coming into my life.
Our love knot is forever tied.
You are my pride.

MA.
7/7/∞

MA's Letter to Jeff

Dear Jeff

Jumping around,
Sprinkling crystals wherever you go.
Splendid like a diamond, you now glow.

You, the Philosopher, the Sage in our rainbow family.
With your pure, innocent heart at the core of your spirituality.
You brought infinite harmony with you into our duality.
We are forever a family.
Happily, Gracefully, Unshakably.
We are forever MA's Rainbow Fam.

I will never forget the first day you arrived,
Wrapped in a rainbow blanket with your big, sparkling eyes;
Always filled with Divine Love and so enthusiastic.
Thank you for coming into my life.
Our love knot is forever tied.
You are my pride.

MA.
7/7/∞

AT THE DAWN OF TIME

Seven years have passed by in the blink of an eye. Grandma MA knows it is time to guide the children back Home—where all creations are in Divine Union, living the eternal love in sacred harmony.

Grandma MA looks at the love notes and knows now is the divine time. "Children, children! The cacao is ready. Come over, my children, bring your blanket. It's time for our weekly snuggles. Let us roast some marshmallows together."

Grandma MA looks up at the moon. In pure silence—there's no sign of children. "Children, children! Come and see the Moon. It's Red tonight. It's time to celebrate. It's story-time." Grandma MA calls her lungs out. But still, there is no sign of any of them.

"Chilllldreeeeeeen! The cacao is ready. We have marshhhmallowwww tonight." Finally, all seven children race over. "Thank you, Cacao Spirit. Thank you, Marshmallow Spirit." Grandma MA murmurs to herself in deep gratitude. Sitting around the fire pit, the children gobble their first cup of cacao, straight down into their tummies, while grabbing a marshmallow with their other hand. "ALL INTO MY BELLY!" Godfrey says, licking the last drop from his cup.

"Tonight is a special night. You must close your eyes during story time. I will bring you inside the story by you all going Into Your HEARTS!" Grandma MA announces with a smile.

"WHAT?"

"WHAATTTTTT!"

"WWHHAAAAATTTT?"

"WWWWHHHHHAAAAATTTTT!" The children scream.

"But Grandma MA, I have no idea how to go into my heart. But I know mine is beating within me all the time ... can you see I am alive?" Sofia asks confidently.

"Maybe Grandma MA is about to give us one of her potions so that we can shrink and go into our hearts," Celeste whispers to the others.

"Or maybe Grandma MA's potion is going to blow up our hearts, so big that we can simply fit inside them," Sofia says, her eyes wild.

"Grandma MA, can I bring my cup of cacao with me while you send me into my heart? And make sure you don't eat up all my marshmallows, promise?" Godfrey says, as he chills on the lounge chair.

"Or maybe there is an enchanted house waiting for us there. Ooooh … I am loving it." Celsa says. She dances around with excitement.

"But Grandma MA," Andrea says. "This seems so boring. I don't even want to go into my heart. Nooo FUN!" He shakes his head, stares at the ground, and furrows his eyebrows.

Jeff jumps around and yells, "But Grandma MA Marshmalloou is still in mah mouuuuuuth … waaaaaiiitttt …" He makes sure everyone hears him.

"I'm absolutely not using ANY of my potions today." Grandma MA laughs as she finishes her cup of cacao. "Don't worry. Just finish up your cacao, and get yourself cozy. NOW!" Looking at the children, Grandma MA feels like they are all mini-MA.

"I will make sure you won't miss out on any of The Divine Treasures," she says.

"Divine Treasures." Andrea screams out. "I'M LOVING IT!"

"Surprise? Not Surprised. By now, I know exactly what the children are thinking at all times." Grandma MA murmurs.

When Grandma MA was about the same age, her mother often told her to go into her heart. "Why is it always all about my heart? I don't know how to go into my heart." Grandma MA often howled back. Grandma MA cannot forget these days. She was clueless about it. "Just go figure it out yourself," her mother told her. Her mother's voice became her initiation.

As Grandma MA grew up, she aspired to be the best mom, the best daughter, the best wife, the best sister, the best friend. She strove to be loving, compassionate, generous, and authentic—all traits rooted in love. She wondered how she could live in her heart as The Love. Daily prayers were all she knew. All her prayers were answered out of the blue through her mystical experience in the Majestic Rainbow World.

Now, Grandma MA lives as its guardian. From the moment she came back from the world of Majestic Rainbow Love, she has dedicated her life to re-creating the Majestic Rainbow Love in reality. Leaving behind the Majestic Rainbow thread here as her Sacred Story.

❊

In stillness, Grandma MA walks over to the fountain and lights up her "One & Only" incense. She summons the entire MA's Rainbow Fam as The Divine Child.

"My Beloved Fellows,
Thank you for holding the space,
Supporting me,
Loving me,
All unconditionally
.
Here I AM, Here I AM, Here I AM
...
As I play my Life Symphony,
As part of The Divine Orchestra.
I AM I
I

.
"

"Grandma!"
"Yes, coming."
"Grandma, Grandma MA!"
"Yes, Yes, I AMMMM COMING."
"Grandma, Grandma, Grandma MAAAA!"
"I-AM-HERE-NOW!"

Not surprisingly, the children are running around, eating and drinking.

"Oh, you two, don't wipe your mouth with your pajamas."

"I certainly wiped it with my full consciousness."

"And I did it with all my love, too, Grandma MA."

"You once said that as long as you do everything with love, all is loved." Andrea says. "See, I remember EVERYTHING you taught me."

Godfrey chimes in. "Oh wait, guys, my body feels like she wants another Marshmallow, wait for meeee. Just one more will do."

"Grandma MA, is this gluten-free, sugar-free, egg-free, dairy-free? I just want to make sure it is because, you know," Celeste says.

"Oh, but I eat raw food only, so please remember, never roast my marshmallow, MA," says Amira.

"For goodness sake. NOT everything in this world can be eaten raw. This marshmallow is the ROOT of a PLANT!" Sofia says with her big eyes.

"Yes, I can. In my reality, I can. I believe I can; I trust I can; I have faith I can."

"No, you can't!"

"Yes, I can."

"No!"

"Yes!"

"Noooo!"

"Yesssss!"

"I wonder who is arguing with Sofia? Do I really need to know? I better just let it be." Grandma MA murmurs.

"Grandma MA! Amira ..." Sofia screams.

"Oh dear, I AM Not Here." Grandma MA answers and laughs.

"Is marshmallow wholesome? I eat wholesome food only. Oh well, this marshmallow does look completely whole to me. Hahaha ... ." Jeff dances in front of Sofia.

"WHAT! Of course it is. Is this even questionable?" With her hands on her waist, Sofia rolls her eyes.

"Oh yeah. Oh yeah ... I love my marshmallow." Jeff says, laughing and shouting.

"The nut-free child is over here, don't forget." Celsa raises her right-hand, hinting.

"Oh well, it is just another typical day for MA's Rainbow Fam. All is well over here." Grandma MA looks up in the sky and shouts, so all can hear.

Grandma takes another deep breath in, slowly spells "P-E-A-C-E. Peeeaaaaccccceeeee." she whispers to herself. "Children. Let's sit around the fire. It's story-time. NOW!" She walks over to each child and hugs them. She lays them down and places her love letters on their hearts. She smiles at each one of them, transmitting her love through her almond-shaped eyes. Then she sings:

"Tonight is the night I know,
As the moon turns red,
The children, all turning seven

...
Now, the moon is red.
So, tonight is the night. I know, I know, I know...
As written,
Now is time to handover The Š."

NOW, YOUR HEART WHISPERS …

In The End,

What

Do

I

Really

Know

?

I Don't Know, I Don't Know, I Don't Know

…

"Once upon a time, I dreamed that one day I would live in a rainbow world of love and unity."

As you comprehend The First Movement, you walk through your first rite of passage to return as the Divine Child, just the way you are. Now, I am one step closer to my dream because of you.

My beloved children, leave your questions here.

From nothingness, you continue your sacred initiation now.

SECOND Š MOVEMENT

THE RECONNECTION THROUGH EXPERIENCES

3	8	1	7	1	8	3
88	4	10	11	10	4	88
44	22	5	2	5	22	44
6	11	2	?	2	11	6
44	22	5	2	5	22	44
88	4	10	11	10	4	88
3	8	1	7	1	8	3

"The Experiences"

*Place your right hand on the square to begin your Second Rite of Passage. Allow the energy to activate your light body."

WHO AM I?
Is This a Question?
Is This Not a Question?

Here & Now

I AM Grandma MA. You are Grandma MA.

I AM Sofia. You are Sofia.

I AM Celeste. You are Celeste.

I AM Amira. You are Amira.

I AM Godfrey. You are Godfrey.

I AM Andrea. You are Andrea.

I AM Celsa. You are Celsa.

I AM Jeff. You are Jeff.

Who AM I? Who Are You?

✢

Even though everyone encompasses the essences of all seven children within us, in different moments, we might resonate with one more than the others. Now, close your eyes and drop your mind into your heart. Out of all seven children, allow yourself to feel into who you are at this moment. Feel into each of the seven children slowly.

Here you ask,

Who AM I?

Who Are YOU?

Now,

YOU are who you are.

As one of the seven children,

YOU journey on with Grandma MA.

THE SACRED INITIATION

From Here, Grandma MA is about to narrate

!

!

!

Grandma MA Narrates Now

...

...

...

"Šhhhh ... just be present here." Grandma MA narrates.

�֍

I scoop a bowl of water from my well and place it at the center of my altar, together with my crystal quartz. I decorate it with my seven rainbow candles and my favorite petals of rose and lotus.

"I know, I know, I AM LOVE. I AM LOVED." Tears roll down my face.

I turn to my left, pick up my hydrangea, and place it in the bowl.

"Here I AM." Even though I wonder who can hear, I believe all creations can hear me. I look around. You all are sitting quietly, observing me. "Can you feel the love within us as a family? Our love is the key to creating magic and miracles in our lives. What you are about to experience is the power of our love as one," I explain.

I turn and walk around you all seven times with my crystal. While I lift my Majestic Wand, "Bi ... BOO!" Rainbow pixie dust manifests around us all. It draws out the lines of the Majestic Rainbow world and dances through the starry sky. Together, we invoke The Eternal Flame—the flame of love and unity.

THE ETERNAL FLAME INVOCATION

"I now invoke The Eternal Flame within me.
Pink, purple, orange, yellow, green and blue.
The Love, The Light, The Life.
I AM, I AM,
I AM I."

"The Eternal Flame"

Using my wand, I paint a dot of rainbow on the moon, and it spins into a mystical door. I look up and cry out, "Here I AM, I AM I AM, I AM I." As the door opens, it showers sparkling diamonds upon us. I see you and the other children, speechless, observing everything unfolding, your jaws dropped down, just as I once was.

"Children, my loves, open your arms wide and receive these lights of love." I point to the light. Sparkling diamonds from the mystical door spin around us all.

Jeff bursts out giggling. "I AM loving it."

You bounce around them and grab a diamond with each hand. You starting shaking; the two diamonds are buzzing, oozing with divine energy.

"Oh my!" Sofia cries, holding the diamonds.

"My love, just close your eyes. Can you hear the river dancing? The birds humming? Your heart pounding? Seven, six, five, four, three, two, one," I whisper.

When you open your eyes, you no longer recognize where you are. All you can feel is a warm glow, expanding and tingling through your body. "Don't hold your breath, my love. Keep breathing," I say to you. "Look around." I gesture to the others to move forward to the woodland glade. It is filled with spirals of iridescent sparks and bubbles. As you look up to the sky, angel wings are flapping everywhere. Horses with horns are galloping toward you from above.

"Oh, the Unicorns!" Celeste shouts. They walk forward softly, touching you and other children's foreheads with their horns. Andrea counts: "One, Two, Three, Four, Five, Six, Seven. One for each of us." When I look at you all, everyone is jumping up and down, feeling excited.

Celsa hugs one of the unicorns. "Squeezy Cheesy." She rubs her face on him and strokes his mane.

"Go. All of you go hop on a unicorn. Try." I lift my Majestic Wand. "Children, NOW ... HERE. Bi ... BOO!" Your bodies begin to feel lighter and lighter, like feathers. Your wings begin to unfurl at your back and spread open gently. Tears roll down my face. "My children, fly, fly, fly with your unicorns. Fly up and down, left and right, all around."

"Jeff! What do you think you are doing, flying so high on the unicorn? Come back." Sofia screams.

"Wait for me!" Godfrey hops on to another unicorn and follows Jeff.

I walk over to Sofia and wrap my arms around her. "All is well, my love. Go fly." I caress her hair.

You and the other children gallop across the sky. The breeze, like feathers, gently strips you down. Your body shrinks slowly. Your hair is shedding; your new baby hair is growing. Suddenly, you and the children burst out in bright white light and transform into a child. You, like the others, become curious with everything in this land. You are ready to explore and experience the magnificence of what is.

As you fly with your newfound freedom on the unicorn, following me gliding across the sky, you spot circles of lights behind the rocks by the stream. Together, we descend to the earth and land. Using all your strength, you push a rock to the right. Sparkling rainbow light bursts out. As you walk closer to the light, you realize that the seven goddesses you have read about in storybooks are the lights themselves.

Hands on your faces, you all scream.

Sofia turns to me, "Are they real?"

"Well ... now, yes, they are real. Remember Lady Mary? Aine? Rati? Isis? Freya? Aphrodite? Quan Yin? All the mystical beings in our bedtime stories are here with you now. They are my fellows. They are welcoming you all with their hearts. Go. Go to them." I say.

As a grandmother, I have always believed that it takes a whole village to grow a well-rounded child. I am so grateful to be connected with my forty-nine fellows. They show you all a way to love through sharing their unique wisdom, while I share mine.

"You might not know where you are heading or what you are about to experience," Quan Yin says, "but you can feel the enchanted love, the grace, and the compassion here. My love, you are perfect just the way you are. Despite any differences between us all, we are one as love,"

"All my seven fellows and I are here to hold the rainbow light as one, to support you on your journeys into the unknown," I add.

"My beloved children, just feel our love from your heart," Aphrodite says.

"As you surrender with your open heart, you uphold your light," Freya says.

"Feel your heart beat and your inner strength. Feel the life force reigniting from the core of your being now," Isis says.

"My love, now you can experience Love from within," Rati says.

"It takes one thought to say 'Yes, I do' and move forward with us," Aine says.

"And be born in me ... ," Lady Mary says.

I lay my hand on each of your hearts, one by one, looking into your eyes. "It all begins through a serendipitous love. From dot to dot, we live The Love." Deep inside, you know you are safe, you know you are loved, and you know you are about to transform. Breathing through all your feelings, you nod. You look at me smiling with a thumbs-up, committing to your journey into the unknown. I smile.

I lift my Majestic Wand. "Bi ... BOO!" All of our wings spread open. We soar and glide through the sky together with my seven fellows. I point down to a waterfall of soft rainbow light and descend. "Here We Are." The blessed air is crisp and sweet. You are astonished by the crystal-clear rainbow waterfall in front of you, where the river thunders down into a vortex-like pond. You feel your whole body vibrate just by staring at this piece of dancing art.

I pick up a hydrangea and, closing my eyes, I place it close to my heart. This place is still magical to me, even after countless times of being here. You and the other children are all giggling and sitting around with big, smiling faces, touching every piece of creation with curiosities and excitements.

"Šhhhh ... just be present here. The best is yet to come." I point at the waterfall. "Your key is to walk through this waterfall," I say. "This is the way, my love. Here is the pathway to the journey within you. My loves, go inside to experience what is."

As I stand in front of the rainbow waterfall, seven of my rainbow fellows stand behind you all in a semicircle, watching your back and upholding our committed roles while emanating our light to you all.

With all our love and light at your back, you follow the other children and move closer to the rainbow waterfall. You turn around and look into my eyes, not knowing what to expect. I smile at you proudly, my face full of tears. I know how it feels—I was once standing where you are now. My heart flooding with feelings, while my mind is blank. I did not know what to think, how I should be feeling, or what was going to happen to me. But with discernment, forgiveness, and compassion, I walked into the unknown.

While I walk to the front of the waterfall with my hydrangea, I bless myself with some of its water and whisper, "Here I AM."

I walk through the waterfall; you all follow. It is dark here; all you can see is a white dot at the center. You grab me tightly, wondering what this is all about. As I place my hydrangea at the dot, a flame ignites and illuminates this place with its rainbow light.

"The Eternal Flame!" Amira exclaims.

"There is one outside on the pond too." Jeff jumps up and down. "The Eternal Flame!"

I am pleased that you all recognize the healing flame of love and unity—The Eternal Flame.

"But Grandma MA, where does The Eternal Flame come from? How did the flame appear without you invoking it?" You ask.

"I, too, don't know how the divine created this flame. I was simply given this as a gift. All I know is, when we are in our heart, it takes only one thought to invoke The Eternal Flame. The purpose of the invocation is to support you, build up your Divine Will to do so," I explain.

"So we can invoke The Eternal Flame whenever and wherever we are? Even without doing the invocation?" Sofia asks.

I nod and gesture to you all to walk into the flame.

As you step into this flame, tears roll down your face. It feels gentle but powerful, deep but soft, transformative, and inclusive. As you shred away your old identities and stories, your being begins to realign into balance as a light being.

Now, I present my "Last Note" to the children:

"In this sacred pilgrimage filled with self-initiations and self-mastery,
I might not see you, you might not see me,
but our heartbeats never fail to reassure us of our gnosis,
our knowing of what is.
Remember our rainbow diamond—
The eternal love of who we truly are,
a love that never dies.
In times of the unknown,
we spread our wings, knowing that
Our rainbow diamond wings will always fly us back to love ... ."

As you look at me again, you and the other children are all shocked, wondering why, all of a sudden, the rainbow light is emanating around me just as it is around the other fellows.

"Grandma MA, how come all of a sudden, the rainbow light is emanating around you? We have never seen that." You ask.

"My love, I have always had my rainbow light around me. You just did not notice. Look at the others, can you see the rainbow light around everyone now?"

"Oh my god!" Godfrey screams with excitement. "We all have a rainbow light around us."

"Through sitting inside The Eternal Flame, you begin to reactivate your rainbow light and your divine eyes. We are all born with a rainbow light and the divine eyes. It is our birthright to experience them in life," I explain.

"But why is this important?" Godfrey asks.

"These are the keys to Co-create United Eternal Sanctuary (CUES) side by side with other ascended beings. It is our eternal soul dream to support our world return to its balance. A new paradigm where love and unity become our reality. You shall gain deeper understanding as you explore the Majestic Rainbow Love," I answer.

"The Majestic Rainbow Love? What's inside?" You wonder.

"As I guide you into this gateway, each one of you will have a different experience," I explain.

Jeff hugs me tightly. "Grandma MA, did you always have this rainbow light around you? I am loving it!"

"Yes, indeed. But most importantly, it is you shining your rainbow light. It is your divine sovereignty to experience the majesty of your divinity in life." I take a deep breath in, knowing not all of you children understand everything I am sharing. But I know this is the way to love.

THE PURPLE DOORWAY

"Children, are you ready to walk inside the Majestic Rainbow Love?" I ask.

"Yes!" You all answer at once.

Celeste panics. "But where are all your forty-nine fellows? Didn't you whisper to me about them just now? There are only seven of them here."

"My love, all my forty-nine fellows are always here with us, even at times when you can't see them. This is their nature. You will meet them when you are meant to," I assure her.

While Celeste is still trying to logically understand my words, I move on and wave my majestic wand. "Bi ... BOO!" The Eternal Flame unveils a gateway with seven doorways in rainbow colors.

Lady Mary walks over and holds my hand. I look at her and nod. We walk toward the first doorway, which is pastel purple, the first ray of the Majestic Rainbow. As I open the door, dusk bursts out in pastel purple light. Lady Mary leads the way in, saying, "Welcome to the Eternal Love, here you remember your 'Once Upon A Dream'."

You all look at me, frowning, and screaming.

"What!"

"WHATTTTT?"

"Šhhhh ... just be present here," I say.

"I have a present here?" Jeff asks and laughs. "Hahaha ... ."

"Where is mine, Grandma MA?" Celeste shakes my arms.

"You will find it out here." I smile at her.

All creations here are in purple. The moment you step in, you are shocked. You see yourself glowing in purple light.

You turn to me and scream, "Grandma MA, why am I all purple? Where AM I?" The moment you start breathing again, you realize I, too, am glowing in purple light. You look up at me and ask, "Who are you? Who Am I?" I hug you and whisper, "Here I AM. I AM I." You hug me tightly.

Lady Mary looks at us and says, "My love, you are inside the first ray of the Majestic Rainbow. Feel the energy of Divine Love cuddling you as you emerge into this eternal purple garden."

You begin to breathe deeply, listening to an angelic voice singing, feeling loved within and without. You become aware of a familiar scent. "Oh, doesn't this smell like your Eternal Love potion, Grandma MA?" Celsa asks.

"Yes, this is the Eternal Love potion. You remember." I said.

"It really smells like jasmine and neroli. It is one of my favorite potions," Celeste says, excited.

"Whenever you come into this garden, you shall find my fellows here. Lady Mary holding the essence of The Eternal Love; Mary Magdalene holding the essence of The Eternal Passion; Green Tara holding the essence of The Eternal Divinity; Black Madonna holding the essence of The Eternal Pearl; Lady Fatima holding the essence of The Eternal Memoir; Lady Nada holding the essence of The Eternal Remembrance; White Tara holding the essence of The Eternal Conception. They are all here eternally, holding up their light and essence for you, so you can remember who you truly are." I whisper to you and the other children.

"Now, Love is eternal. There is no beginning and no end here. To understand eternity, compassion is your key," says White Tara.

Looking around this purple garden, you feel you are completely relaxed with no thoughts. It is simply breathtaking. You feel you can sit here all day long just to breathe in the Love. Now, you are enjoying this moment here. "Children, you do not need to know how you will navigate within this Majestic Rainbow gateway. You will find your way through your remembrance. Now, let me walk you to Mary Magdalene," I say.

As you pass all the jasmine and neroli flowers, you can't help but pick a couple of them. Looking at your beautiful bouquet, you know you are loved. I smiled looking at you.

"Come, my love." Mary Magdalene sings gently. As you receive her essence, your passion ignites. Now you walk toward Black Madonna, who is holding a treasure box with a note: 'The Divine Treasure.' When she opens it, beautiful amethyst crystal hearts, unlike anything you have seen before, appear. Inside each of the hearts, there is a pearl. As you and the other children receive it, you all place it close to your heart. You begin to feel the pulse of this living heart, emanating pure love. You know this is a manifestation of the divine heart.

"My beloved ones, it is time you reclaim your purest essence and be The Love. This Heart is the key, forgiveness is the way, and you are the gift. So it is, so it is, so it is." We all hear a whisper from the crystal hearts.

Suddenly, a thread of light shoots into your heart from the crystal heart. You feel your heartbeat, my heartbeat, and the heartbeats of all creations unified as one, beating within you. When you look around at other children, everyone is in a state of grace.

"Everything here seems to be intangible." Andrea looks up at Black Madonna.

"Everything within the Majestic Rainbow Love is tangible and intangible. This is love, my love," Black Madonna says.

"But why?" Amira asks.

"It is just what it is, my love," Black Madonna explains.

You and the other children walk slowly toward Lady Fatima. She smiles at you all. The moment your eyes connect with hers, flashes of memories flood back. "Yes, I remember, I remember now ... ," Celeste cries out.

As you turn around, you see Lady Nada walking toward you. You exclaim, "I remember now."

You turn toward White Tara, reading aloud the essence she holds, 'The Eternal Conception.' "What is it? I Don't Know, I Don't Know, I Don't Know ... ."

As White Tara anoints you and the others with The Eternal Love potion, she says, "Congratulations, my dears, now you all realize you don't know ... Here, you are grace."

I see you, and the other children looking at me with a frown. So I say, "Šhhhh ... just be present here," and smile.

"Taste it," says White Tara.

"Ooooooh. It does taste like lavender," Godfrey says excitedly. "Am I right?"

"I Don't Know ... . I don't know how you feel it tastes like, but You do KNOW." White Tara smiles.

Sofia looks at me again to see what I have to say about this. So, I repeat, "Šhhhh ... just be present here," and gesture for you and the other children to say good bye to all my fellows here and follow me again.

And within my heart I know...

Here, you feel...
You remember your compassion,
You connect with forgiveness,
You create grace from within,
You realize you are the love.
"Now, I know I am loved," Grandma MA whispers.
"But where is my Home?" Your heart wonders ...

The Blue Doorway

As I come out of the purple garden, I look at you and the other children. You are all jumping around, feeling excited. Even though you have questions arising from within, you are eager to explore more.

"Let's go, I AM ready!" Godfrey yells.

"Oh yes! Go, go, go." Jeff laughs.

With my heart full of joy, I walk toward Aine who is holding the essence of the Sacred Crib. I take her hands in mine. We smile at each other and walk toward the next doorway. I open the second doorway, which is pastel blue—the second ray of the Majestic Rainbow. As the door opens, light radiates out in blue. I can't help but stare at it for a moment, while Aine leads the way in. She says, "Welcome to your Innate Healing. Here you bathe in love; you heal through love. Through here, you shall find your way."

Looking around, you are amazed by the blue light surrounding you.

When Celeste looks down at herself, she is shocked. She screams, "Grandma MA! Why am I in blue? Where AM I?" Suddenly, Celeste realizes I am glowing in blue, too. She comes close, looks into my eyes and asks, "Who are you? Who Am I?"

I wrap around her, and whisper in her ear, "Here I AM." Then, I hold your hand and smile at you. You can hear the music of a string trio and the sound of the river dancing. Despite the unknown in front of you, you feel immense healing energy surrounding you. As you breath in deeply, these healing vibrations calm and nourish you. I walk down the stairs slowly. You and the other children follow. The smell of roses is thick all around. Rose petals and candle lights are dangling everywhere, lighting the way.

Celeste runs over and hugs me. "This smells like the Enchanted Cauldron potion. My favourite potion, Grandma MA."

"Of course it is," I whisper. I smile.

As you hit the bottom of the stairs, you see patches of roses and patchouli surrounding a Sacred Crib at the center of the room. In front of you, standing with Aine, there are six other fellows: Airmed, holding the essence of the Sacred Balm; Danu, holding the essence of the Sacred Chalice; Ceridwen, holding the essence of the Sacred Well; Olwen, holding the essence of the Sacred Cloak; Rhiannon, holding the essence of the Sacred Fountain; and Brigid, holding the essence of the Sacred Key. They are standing here inside the room at the seven corners.

You can't help but look at me in surprise. "They are all real?"

I smile. "Šhhhh ... just be present here."

This room is like a cauldron. You can feel its alchemical healing power.

"I want to stay here forever," Godfrey says, and lies on the floor.

Celsa pushes her way to me gently and whispers, "Where is my present now, Grandma MA?"

I say, "Šhhhh ... just be present here."

Airmed walks forward and says, "Through your devotions, you create your enchantments." She anoints her Sacred Balm on you.

Danu walks toward the Sacred Crib and pours her essence inside, sprinkling roses and patchouli all over it. The Crib is now filled with roses and patchouli, glowing in iridescent pink and pastel green sparkles. She says, "Come to me, my beloved children. Take a sip from my Sacred Chalice."

You hesitate; look around to the others. Suddenly you all burst into laughter.

Jeff walks over laughing. "This is so funny. Hahahaha ...." He takes his first sip. "Woooooo ... this tastes like Bergamot. I want MORE!"

Now you and the other children are all sipping from the crib.

"I am loving it. I think it tastes like rose." Amira smiles at me.

You love the taste and cant help to take another sip from it. Ceridwen walks over and puts her hand on your shoulder and kiss you from behind. She puts you and the other children inside the crib. "Lie down and enjoy this for a moment," she says softly. "Just rest and feel, my love." You feel your skin softening, your hair shining, your body glowing. As if you are rebirthing into a newborn baby."

You listen to a trio of musicians—violin, viola, and cello—while inhaling the divine smell of the Innate Healing potion. You look around and see the seven fellows standing around all of you, forming a circle of light with diamonds flying everywhere inside the ring, all vibrating with Divine Love. As you look down upon your naked self, you realize you are shining, eminating your rainbow light like the rest of us.

"Really? Am I just daydreaming?" You look up at me, shedding tears.

"No." I smile and carry you and the other children out of the crib.

Olwen, from the far end, walks over with her Sacred Cloak. She cloaks you all with her essence and hugs you in silence. You feel her transmitting her love to you through her heartbeats. You feel your heartbeats are synchronizing with hers. While you are still enjoying this moment,

Rhiannon waves you over. "Finally, I get to meet you all, children." She pours her essence onto each one of you. "From this moment on, you are a Fountain of Love. You are the alchemy." She offers you all some roses and patchouli to add to the bouquets.

Andrea stumbles over to me and proudly presents his unique posy, so I lean forward and breathe it in with a big smile. I know, beyond your logical mind, you feel the love all around you from within. Now, my heart is in bliss because of you.

I tap on to your shoulder and gesture you and the other children to follow me. I walk back to the stairs. Standing in front of the stairs is Brigid. She is holding the treasure box with her Sacred Keys inside. One for each of you all. The moment you hold the key, it transforms into iridescent bubbles. You touch them, and they pop.

"MA! They ... all ... pop and transform into nothingness." Sofia yells. You all turn to me with a big question mark on your face, not knowing what to ask.

I say, "What is it?"

You and the other children all reply, "I Don't KNOW!"

I smile "You've got it now. Now you realize you don't know."

Brigid looks into all of you children's eyes and says, "My beautiful children, just like every one of us, you have an innate healing ability within. It is in this state of "I Don't Know", you begin to find your healing at every level. Knowing that you have a deep inner knowing within the state of "I Don't Know." Yes, you know. Yes, you do know."

They look at each other and whisper, "But, I Don't Know, I Don't Know, I Don't Know ... ."

Brigid smiles. "Yes. The key to 'I Know' is 'I Don't Know.'"

As you breathe in the wisdom, you place both hands on your heart with gratitude. In silence, I hear Celeste whispering to herself, "All I know is, I AM love."

You whisper to me. "Now, I know I AM love."

I walk over to Brigid, and, in tears, we hug. As you and the other children are saying goodbye to my fellows here, I ask you all, "Where do you think we are heading next?"

Jeff walks forward and says proudly, "I DON'T KNOW!"

"I Don't Know too," Celsa adds.

You all repeat, "I Don't Know," and giggle.

I smile in bliss because I know—you and the other children are all ready to move forward.

Suddenly, a mist of rainbow fog rushes toward us. None of us can see a thing. So, I summon to you all, "Spread your wings now!" As I spread mine, the mist subsides. When I look around, I realize I am back at The Eternal Flame next to the waterfall. One by one, I see you all are back here, giggling and hugging one another.

I look at you and smile, "Šhhhh ... just be present here." And within my heart I know...

Here, you feel ...
You remember your enchantments,
You connect with devotion,
You create alchemy from within,
You realize you are the healing.
"Now, I know I am loved." Grandma MA whispers to herself.
"But where is my Home?" Your heart wonders ...

The Green Doorway

As I walk to the waterfall and bless myself with its water, I see Rati, who holds the essence of the Magnificent Egg. She is waiting for us in front of the third doorway, which is in pastel green—the third ray of the Majestic Rainbow. I walk over and hold hands with Rati. As I open the door, the specular green light strikes into our hearts. Our bodies vibrate with Divine Love. Now, Rati leads the way in, and says, "Welcome to your Gnosis Wisdom."

As you walk inside this doorway, the sound of a sitar and the familiar smell of the Gnosis Wisdom potion welcome you. Everything around you looks like a matrix embedded with light codes, as if you are standing in the middle of the galaxy.

Suddenly, a tornado of Chi swirls over us. Everyone flies and swirls, until just as suddenly, gravity drags us down. We all land on our knees.

"Oh my goodness!"

"What Da?"

"Gosh. What is this?"

"Grandma MA!"

"Oooooo ..."

You and the other children all scream. I take a deep breath in and say, "Šhhhh ... just be present here. Do you know where you are now?"

"I DON'T KNOW!" You all answer.

"Wisdom comes from experiences within." I smile and look around. Ginger candies are sparkling everywhere. I put one in my mouth and you follow. "Ooooh, this is ginger candy? ... NO WAY! Did they also put cinnamon, pepper, nutmeg, and cardamom in it, MA?" you ask.

Godfrey fills his mouth with the candies, giving me a thumbs up. "I want more," he says.

I wink.

Andrea looks around to see what else he can find. He yells, "Present, I SEE YOU waiting for me."

"Šhhhh ... just be present here," I smile at him. I gesture to you all to follow me and Rati. We walk forward. We turn left, we turn right. After many turns, we arrive at a river, under a dome where my other fellows are waiting for us on a boat—Parvati, holding the essence of the Magnificent Prism; Saraswati, holding the essence of the Magnificent Crown; Kali, holding the essence of the Magnificent Chamber; Adti, holding the essence of the Magnificent Bell; Lakshmi, holding the essence of the Magnificent Lamp; and Shakti, holding the essence of the Magnificent Feather. You and the children are feeling excited again. You jump and giggle with the others. So, I turn around and say, "Still ... Šhhhh ... just be present here." I smile.

As we get on the boat, Rati hands over some egg-shaped floaties for us to wear as protection. We all begin to row. Slowly, steadily, we row and flow along the river. When I look at you, I see you become curious about everything you are experiencing and the coming unknown. As we row, our surroundings become darker until the boat stops in pure darkness. I can't see you, and you can't see me. Tingling sensations move through our bodies. Each cell is dancing, expanding as if it has become a living matrix. Our heartbeats are all that we can hear here.

Being in this unknown of what is, Lakshmi opens her treasure box. An Aurora green light illuminates the sky. From the aurora, an almond shape unveils and spins above us.

"The EYE! The All-Seeing Eye," Amira shouts.

"I am ready for love, to love and live love now." Godfrey yells.

"Blessed you are, my love," Rati says. "This is your divine eye. May you experience our world from the eye of Love now. With this eye, you can see beyond any veils. You can witness the magnificence of the divine."

You all give me a thumbs up and look around again. You are all electrified by the green light swimming across the sky.

"Isn't this called the Northern Light?" Celsa whispers to me.

"Yes, one of its many names indeed." I wink.

Excited, you all point at the light.

Andrea says, "Present, I SEE YOU waiting for me."

"Šhhhh ... just be present here," I say. I smile.

Now, Lakshmi dips her finger in her elixir and draws a circle around each of you and the other children. "Light up the light within you," she says. Instantly, you feel warmth kindle in your core. A glow arises and illuminates your entire being.

All of you are shocked; your bodies freeze instantly. You and the other children look at me. I walk over and say, "All is well. My Loves. This is your true nature." I wrap my love around you all, one by one.

"Are you serious?" Celeste squashes my face.

I clasp her to my heart and tickle her. Everybody cracks up.

"Children, Children. Šhhhh ... just be present here," I say.

"Not me! It's because of Celeste." Amira points at Celeste.

"Nooo ... It's NOT ME!" Celeste points at me. "It's Grandma MA!"

So, I smile and repeat, "Šhhhh ... just be present here."

"Oh yes!" Jeff giggles.

Jeff's giggles become the opening symphony of Lakshmi's ceremony. As Lakshmi pours her essence into the river, the river turns into a stream of sparkling glitter stars.

Kali steps up and cuts across the stream with her finger. The Magnificent Chamber establishes. "Here We are," she says.

Parvati stands up and places her Magnificent Prism at the center of the chamber, and says, "Here we birth and rebirth through our creativities."

Shakti waves her feather and paints across the chamber with it. "Here is our vision; now we see." The Eye unveils inside the prism, and clove flowers bloom as eyelashes around it instantly.

Aditi walks over to the center of The Eye and rings her bell. She waves us over, "Now, we are One as I. Through your creativities, you unlock your visions."

As you walk through the lashes of clove blossoms, you invoke your inner creativities. You pick a few flowers to add to your bouquet, and look at me with your smiling face. You say, "I know I AM loved."

Slowly, we walk together to the center of the eye. On our way, we realize our entire bodies are covered with glittering lights. As we step into the center of the prism—on The Eye, we see reflections of ourselves.

"Stand here with me, around The Eye," I say.

You and the other children stand in a circle, staring at each other.

Nothing happens. You all look at me.

"Now, let's cuddle to experience our power of Love and Unity," I say. I smile.

The moment we cuddle up, a burst of light from The Eye radiates out in rainbow aurora. My heart fills with bliss; my eyes fill with tears. I scream in excitement, "YOU DID IT! Children, You DID it!" I put my hands on my heart, fall to my knees crying, saying, "Oh My Loves, we did it! We DID IT!" All of you run toward me and hug me. We wipe each other's tears, caressing each other's faces.

"But, what did we just do?" Celsa asks.

"What do you think you have just done?" I ask.

"I Don't Know?" you answer.

So I continue, "All I felt is the power of our love as one. This is what matters." I turn and realize Saraswati is waiting for us with her treasure box.

I gesture to you all to go to her. She unseals her treasure box, and rainbow sparkles gush out from the box. You flinch. I catch you from behind, pointing up to the sky. "Here I AM, my love." You see diamond crowns hanging overhead. You reach out with your left hand.

"Bi ... Boo! The Magnificent Crown. Dupi-Dupi-Doo ..." Saraswati waves her majestic wand, and she crowns you all, one by one.

I see your tears flow down your cheeks. "Why am I crying, Grandma MA. Am I alright?"

"You do not need to understand everything in this world logically," I say. "Crying is just a way our body expresses emotions. Our tears are a mechanism to empty our emotions, similar to our sweat glands. Don't ever judge your tears. Embrace them all, my love."

You and the other children receive your final blessings from my fellows here as a gesture of goodbye. Then, we walk over to The Eye and sit. We snuggle up and giggle.

"Here we end, Here we begin." I say.

Together, we invoke The Eternal Flame. As we all sit in the flame again, our reality transforms, and the aurora spins around us. I know our new reality is about to unveil itself. Finally, we find ourselves back at the The Eternal Flame, next to the waterfall. None of You can conceptualize what just happened, but I know this marks the beginning of a new life ahead of you all.

And within my heart I know ...

Here, you feel ...
You remember your origin,
You connect with insights,
You create visions from within,
You realize you are the wisdom.
"Now, I know I am loved," Grandma MA whispers to herself.
"But where is my Home?" Your heart wonders ...

THE YELLOW DOORWAY

I stroll to the waterfall and bless myself with its water again. I look around and utter. "I AM Home." I wonder what is in place for you and the other children moving forward in the next doorway. I turn around. I see Isis holding her essence of the Immortal Seal, smiling at me. "Are you ready, my love?" she says.

I nod. She takes my hand. I open the fourth doorway. It is pastel yellow—the fourth ray of the Majestic Rainbow. As I open the door, a spectacular sunshine-colored smoke bursts forth with a pungent aroma of The Immortal potion. I feel I am swimming amongst the hyssop, galbanum, frankincense, and myrrh.

"Godfrey, Godfrey! Your favorite potion." Celsa says excitedly.

Andrea yells. "Oh, he just ran inside already. Godfrey, come back!"

I look at Isis. We both laugh. "Welcome to your Divine Will," she says to you all. She smiles and leads the way in, "Godfrey, my darling, welcome to your Divine Will, just in case you couldn't hear me." Isis winks at me.

You look around and spot six of my fellows waiting for us here.

Andrea asks Isis, "Who are they?"

Isis smiles and gestures for you all to walk inside.

Andrea turns to me and asks, "Who?" He points at my six fellows.

"Šhhhh ... just be present here." I look at him and gesture to him to follow the others.

As you walk in, Bastet, who holds the essence of the Immortal Womb, sprays you all with her essence.

"Here I AM, my love," she says, and sprays again.

The yellow mist cleanses your aura and imbues it with yellow glitter. Curious, you open your mouth to taste it.

Sofia tastes it. "This has frankincense in it. Isn't this the tea you always brew, Grandma MA?"

I nod and smile. I know this marks the beginning of you and the other's rebirth, reclaiming all your sovereignty. Looking across the landscape, I wave to my fellows. Hathor, who holds the essence of the Immortal Thread; Nephthys, who holds the essence of the Immortal Charm; Nut, who holds the essence of the Immortal Wings; Renenet, who holds the essence of the Immortal Halo; Maat, who holds the essence of the Immortal Scepter.

Looking around, you notice you are standing in a desert filled with plants. Diamond sparkles skitter across the golden sand. You bend down for a closer look at the sparkling diamonds, only to realize they are diamond flames. All of you children jump and play excitedly with these flames.

"For sure, I am adding these diamond flames to my bouquet," You say excitedly.

The other children immediately follow you.

Looking at all of your bouquets, my heart fills with gratitude and love. "Okay, Okay, children. All your bouquets are gorgeous. Do you know each of the diamond flames is a prayer to our world?" I wave my Majestic Wand toward the sand. "Bi ... Boo!" Another flame ignites. "And this flame is my prayer to you all—to live in harmony with all of creations from now on."

I put my wand on your hand and gesture to you to make a prayer, too. "Bi ... Boo! Speak from your heart now, so all creations can hear ... ." As you pray silently, I see your flame reignite. I blow a kiss onto your flame, to seal it with my love. Everyone can feel the divine power bursting out of the flame, touching our hearts. Simply by being amongst the flames, you feel your life force, power, and passion reigniting, like a roaring dragon fire deep within you—as if you and the flame are one.

"Present, present, come to me pleeaaassseeeee ... ." Wondering who is speaking, you look up to realize everyone is gone. You spot Bastet and the other children surrounding Hathor at the far end of the garden in front of you. "Who was speaking?" you murmur and wonder. You decide to move forward anyway and stroll across the desert to reunite with the others. Hathor waves, gesturing you to come over. When you arrive, you see the other children are playing with a thread of flames. Hathor smiles and wraps her arm around you. "Here is yours, my love." She pulls out a thread of flames and swings it across the sand. The thread weaves into a circle of light. She kneels and looks into your eyes. "Do you want to blow some bubbles?"

You nod. She gestures for you to exhale through the circle and experience the magic. You take a deep breath in and blow ... Rainbow bubbles gush out.

"Look at these photos on the bubbles. Can you find yourself there?"

Excitedly, you take a closer look. In each of them, you find photos of yourself at different ages and at different times.

"Grandma MA, I see us roasting marshmallows over here." Godfrey yells.

Jeff jumps up and down. "Grandma MA, I see myself wrapped around with my rainbow Love-Love blanket! My favorite Love-Love."

"Grandma MA, I see us drinking cacao in our garden." Sofia says.

"Now, it is time to pop the bubbles to release all your old stories to make space for new ones. Children, whenever you feel challenged in letting go, your divine willpower assists you in overcoming all obstacles," I say. Like others, you are dancing around, popping bubbles, giggling, while letting go of old stories that no longer serve you. I know you are rebirthing. Now is the perfect time. You are ready to unleash who you truly are in our world. With mixed emotions, I begin to sing, "Let it go ... Let it go ... Let it go ... ." Knowing what we have lived by, and that "Love and Unity" has shaped you into who you are now, profound gratitude bursts from deep within me. Looking at you and the other children, I know I AM loved. Just when I wonder if it is time for me to pop some bubbles, Hathor walks up to me, holding the circle of light.

"My love, let's blow a bubble together, shall we?" She winks. I nod and throw sand at her like we used to. We hug and laugh. Together holding hands, we take a deep breath in and blow through the circle of light she is holding.

I wink. I Hop, I Jump, I Hum. "Wow. My biggest bubbles ever." When I take a closer look at the shimmering bubbles, I see memories of my time with my rainbow fellows streaming inside the bubble. "I guess now is the time. What do you think?" I say.

Hathor gives me her cheeky smile "One, two, three."

We both pop the bubble and jump onto each other. Laughing and rolling on the sand, we cry out aloud, "We Did IT!"

"Are they drunk?" Jeff walks over and pokes my face.

We both laugh. "Yes, we are drunk in love, my love," Hathor replies.

Jeff wears an angry face. With his hands on his waist and his chin up high, he says, "No more drinking. You grownups!" He leans into me, and puts his face on mine, shaking his head.

As we sit up laughing, we see Renenet is already standing next to you with her treasure box.

Andrea interrupts. "Can I open it? I want to open it. Present, present, come to me pleeaaassseeeee ..."

"Šhhhh ... just be present here," I say.

Renenet opens her treasure box.

Celeste points above your head, "SEE. You have a HALO!" You try to look up and around. Soon you realize everyone has a halo above them now.

Renenet explains, "My children, this is your Immortal Halo and it has an infinite source of power; it glows whenever you stand in your own power."

"Whattt?" Amira frowns.

"WHATT!" Celeste exclaims.

"WHATTTTT?" Jeff shouts.

I know you might not fully understand the complex meaning behind it right now, but I know your understanding of this will mature as time goes by. Just when you're all playing and giggling with your Halos, Nephthys walks over in silence and places a charm around your and the other children's necks.

"What have you just put around my neck, Nephthys?" Celsa asks. "You are cheeky."

"I AM loving it! Don't you, Celsa?" Andrea exclaims.

"Well, I believe this can protect me." Sofia says.

"Protect you from WHATTTTT?" Jeff laughs. "In my opinion, this beautifies me. It makes me happy. It's Party Time! Yeah."

"NO! Not my truth." Sofia shakes her head and walks away.

Nephthys smiles and explains, "Children, now it is time to reclaim your full sovereignty right through your rebirthing. This process of your rebirth requires you to keep experimenting in life and with life. Since the dawn of time, life itself is an experiment to expand the love within us beyond our imagination."

I walk over, holding both Sofia and Jeff's hands, facing the other children. "My beloved children, just remember you are loved, and you are love."

I pause and look up to the sky. "And always believe in love." When I look at you and the other children again, you are all experimenting with the charms. Now I witness the charms on your necks transform into light and melt into each of your bodies.

Nut walks over slowly. She wraps her wings around me, smiling, looking at you and the other children. "We are all love."

Maat appears behind me suddenly, holding her scepters high.

Andrea jump up and down. "Is that our present here?"

"Use it with Love." Maat gives an Immortal Sceptre to each one of you.

I smile. "All divine creations are rooted in love, right?"

"YES. And it creates resurrections from within you. So let us all hold it up high now." Maat smiles.

With all of our sceptres, we form a circle around Maat and begin to dance.

"Oh yea, it's party time!" Jeff yells.

You all are moving your bodies, jumping, hopping, and dancing around. As Maat hums—Da-dum-da-dum ... da-dum-da-dum ... da-dum-da-dum ... Nut grows taller and taller until her head hits the clouds. Vibrant rock roses sprout up suddenly from the desert sand. Birds fly from all directions above us, singing, and join us. When all the rock roses have flourished and the sun is setting, we are feeling the love within and without. We are all in bliss.

"I am tired now, I need to rest," Celsa says.

"Me too," Celeste adds.

So, Nut bends over. "Come. Come, all of you, come sit beneath me."

You drag your body over and sit next to the other children under Nut's belly. You look up. "Wooow, what is this, Grandma MA?" You witness her belly transform into the cosmic galaxy.

You and the other children are all glued to the ground, watching auroras flow in the galaxy inside Nut's belly. Suddenly, we feel a surge of gravity from the ground pulling us down. In a blink, all of us are sucked into a pitch-dark void of nothingness. We twirl and tumble, not knowing what is going on. Your heart is about to pop out. Nut shouts "The Wings!" She sprinkles her essence on you all.

I shout. "Your wings! Remember, together with the faith you hold, your rainbow diamond wings will always fly you back Home."

Within this void of nothingness now, I cannot hear a sound, I cannot see a light, I cannot feel anything. So, I know we are all rebirthing now. With my divine will, I relax and soften my body. I focus on my breath. I allow my body to swing and flow with what is. In no time, I land on my knees and lie down at The Eternal Flame next to the waterfall. "Children, are you all here?" I yell and roll over slowly to check on you all.

"Here I AM, What has just happened?" Sofia asks.

"Here I AM, What was that?" Celeste asks.

"Here I AM, Where were we?" Amira asks.

"Here I AM, When did I arrive?" Godfrey asks.

"Here I AM, How did I come back?" Andrea asks.

"Here I AM, Why, Why, Why?" Celsa asks.

"Here I Am, Whatttt. Whaaaat! Whaaaaaaattt?" Jeff asks.

I get up slowly and walk to you all saying, "All is well now. Just breathe from here." And within my heart I know...

Here, you feel ...
You remember your sovereignty,
You connect with your faith,
You create resurrections from within,
You realize you are the divine will.
"Now, I know I am loved." Grandma MA whispers to herself.
"But where is my Home?" Your heart wonders...

THE ORANGE DOORWAY

As I walk over to the waterfall again and bless myself with its water, I see Freya talking to you and the other children.

I wave to Freya. "Here I AM." She gestures for me to walk over to the pastel orange doorway, which is the fifth ray of the Majestic Rainbow. As I reunite with her, you all are still recovering from the journey in the yellow doorway. Freya asks, "Children, Are you ready?"

You rub your eyes, yawn, and take a deep breath. I walk forward to hold Freya's hand and open the fifth door. You all follow and gather around this doorway. When I open the door, a mixed swirl of tangerine color and golden light radiates out. Freya leads the way, sprinkling stars everywhere. She says, "Welcome to your Humility." "HUH?" Jeff frowns and looks at me.

I smile.

Celsa whispers in my ear. "What is Humility?"

"Experiments." I state firmly.

"WHAT?"

"My love, self-realizations don't come from our logical minds. They come directly from our hearts. Faith is needed in times of the unknown. Our faith is activated through the stillness. The experiments in life have been my secret to understand Humility," I explain.

Celsa nods and follows the rest of the children.

"Grandma MA, this smells like my favorite potion—The Infinite Light, isn't it?" Andrea asks.

"Yes, my love."

"Ahhhhh ... I just love this smell of pine, spruce, peppermint, eucalyptus, rosemary ... What else?"

I smile at Andrea. "Šhhhh ... just be present here."

I gesture to you all to walk inside the majestic forest. This forest is filled with tall pine and spruces, with a river flowing across the landscape.

We look tiny standing next to the trees. As they sway, their ethereal flute sound makes your heart sing. You drop down onto the grass and look up to the sky. Orange-colored clouds are floating above, like a cotton candy in the sky.

"It's dreamy here, I am loving it, Grandma MA. Now, I AM peace," says Jeff.

Celeste leaps around under a tree. "I am free!"

Godfrey, dash around the forest, playing a treasure hunter.

Amira jumps onto the tallest tree and wraps herself around it. Shaking it, she whispers, "Bi ... Boo! Presents, presents, please pour all over me NOW."

Showers of rainbow pixie dust and pine cones pour down onto Celsa instantly. She laughs and twirls around with her arms wide open, receiving them.

I smile at her and whisper, "Šhhhh ... just be present here."

In silence, you and other children add a few pine cones and spruce leaves to your bouquet. You place your nose inside the bouquet. "Simply Divine."

Sofia smiles, looking at her bouquet. "What a beauty I have here with me."

We continue to walk and walk. In front of us, we see the ocean and the horizon. There, an Ark is waiting for us. Snotra, who holds the essence of the Benevolent Ark, stands at the entrance, waving at us. She welcomes us. Forehead to forehead, she touches all seven of you children. "Here I AM, my loves." She gestures for everyone to come onto the Ark, and to move forward together.

As the Ark sails across the ocean, I rest quietly at the back of the Ark, enjoying my alone time.

You and the children suddenly all scream and yell.

"It's a ice-land!" Jeff yelled

Sofia calls me over. "Grandma MA, we have arrived. Look."

When I walk over, I see Eir, who holds the essence of the Benevolent Realm, standing in front of a river, waving at us. One by one, we hop onto the ice-land.

"Godfrey! Don't lick the ice." Sofia yells.

Godfrey cannot resist. He sticks his tongue out and licks the ice.

Sofia yells again. "Godfrey! You should not lick the ice."

"So Spicy." "It tastes like PEPPERMINT!" Godfrey yells with a cheeky smile.

Sofia turns around, shaking her head.

Eir walks over to Godfrey. "All is well, my love," she says, and pats him with her Left Hand from behind. "Let's play now, shall we?" Eir takes Godfrey's hand and blows on his index finger. A flame ignites.

Godfrey's jaw drops, he stares at his finger. "My fingerrrr ... ."

Eir giggles, holding his finger and drawing a dot of flame in the air. In a flash, this dot transforms into a humongous magnifying glass.

Immediately, you stick your nose to the glass and look through it. Through your heart, you see another world inside the magnifying glass. A world in pure rainbow colors. There is a lush forest with rivers, and a crystal clear ocean. This pristine landscape is spread with millions of transparent cosmic matrixes filled with rainbow diamond lights. Here, there are advanced technological creations beyond your imagination. Looking inside the magnifying glass, you and the other children drop into stillness, as if there is no time or space. I can feel you all are awed by this world.

"What in the world!" Jeff exclaims.

Sofia turns and looks at Eir. "This is truly an innovative and integrated way of living. Combining the ancient and modern way of living, all in one world."

Celeste walks over to Eir. "How can we get there?" she asks.

"My love, Dream from the Love; Create a world of Love and live Love," Eir explains. She points to Hel, who holds the essence of the Benevolent Float. Hel is waiting for us.

While Celsa and Jeff's faces are still glued to the magnifying glass, Godfrey walks over to hug me and says "Now, I know I AM Loved."

I smile at him. "May your humility bring you deep and far into life. You light up our world. Children, Let's go now." I grab both Celsa and Jeff's hands, and walk toward Hel while the others follow.

"Hey, where is my present?" Jeff asks.

Amira pulls his hand, "Šhhhh ... You cannot talk like that."

"Why can't I?" Jeff walks away.

"All is loved. All is well, my love." I hug Jeff while smiling at Amira.

In silence, Hel is drawing a circle in the air with his fingers, forming a portal filled with diamond sparkles. You are shocked and look up at Hel. "Can I do this one day?"

"My love, your unique set of divine gifts is already within you. In the name of love, all is possible," Hel replies.

You nod and continue to look around.

Sofia points at the portal. "Wow ... Look over there."

Floats are flying straight at us from the portal.

"Now is the time to live from your heart. Through the Benevolent float, you flow to the world you just saw. The world of love and unity; the world where all creations live in sacred harmony," Hel explains. You jump onto a float quickly, eager to experiment with it.

"Wait a minute, children. Look over there. See who is here with us." Hel points at the three fellows who have just walked over with their treasure box—Idun, who holds the essence of the Benevolent Balloon; Gefjun, who holds the essence of the Benevolent Arrow; Sjöfn, who holds the essence of the Benevolent Carousel.

Idun smiles. "Here are the three divine gifts from us."

"The Balloon, The Arrow, and The Carousel," Gefjun adds.

"But what are we supposed to do with these?" Celsa asks.

"What do you think you can do with these?" Sjofn looks into Celsa's eye with a smile.

"I Don't Know."

"Great start. Now, begin to experiment with them." Sjofn makes sure you all have received your gifts and hugs you.

Idun, who has been standing next to you, bends down to look into your eyes. "My love, go experiment in life and with life. It is where divine miracles are bestowed."

"I wonder if these gifts will bring me Home," Sofia ask.

Idun smiles. "My love, You Are Home."

"This is my Home?" Sofia ask again.

"Now, Here. You are Home," Sjofn answers.

Andreas skips over with his tongue out. "Oh My! Now, I am finally feeling I AM Home."

I smile, and give him a thumbs up.

"How about me? Where is My Home?" Celeste asks.

"How about me? Me, too. I want to go home." Celsa says.

"Me, Too!" Sofia says.

"The moment when all questions dissolve, you are Home." I wink. I lift Sofia's hand and place it on my heart. "Now. Here. I AM Home." Sofia nods. So we hold hands and walk forward with the other children.

My fellows are standing on both sides, saying goodbye to us while celebrating our new beginning in front of us. They begin to wave their hands to say goodbye and sing our song—"*We Are Home*". "The Rainbow is shining, flowing, and birthing through us all. As I celebrate you, you celebrate me. We live, we live in sacred harmony ... ."

"Off we go to the rainbow land. I feel that's my Home." Andrea jumps onto his float. "Down! Float down the river."

You and the other children follow. You are all singing out loud, feeling excited about what you all have just experienced within this doorway.

As we sing, we flow along the river. In no time, we all slide over the rainbow waterfall and return to The Eternal Flame.

Jeff cackles. "Hahaha ... I AM Loving it! This has to be a new beginning for us all."

I look at Jeff with a wink. "Do you really know what 'new beginning' means?"

"I Don't Know!" Jeff says. "But do I need to know?"

I smile and kiss his cheek.

I walk slowly and sit inside The Eternal Flame, closing my eyes.

Here, my heart speaks aloud, "Once upon a time, I dreamed that one day I would live in a rainbow world of love and unity." I whisper to myself, "Yes, I remember." When I open my eyes again, you are all sleeping soundly. And within my heart I know ...

Here, you feel ...
You remember your stillness,
You connect with peace,
You create new beginnings from within.
You realize you are the light.
"Now, I know I am loved." Grandma MA whispers to herself.
"But where is my Home?" Your heart wonders ...

The Pink Doorway

I walk over to you and the other children and give you each a hug. Looking at you, I bend down to kiss your cheek. You open your eyes and look at me with tears rolling down your face. Even though I have a million words I want to share, I caress your face in silence. I know silence is one of the most sacred ways to witness divine miracles. Forehead to forehead, I touch you with my love. I wipe your tears away with my Left Hand, knowing you know you are loved.

"Grandma MA." Celsa rubs her eyes. "Where are we?"

I caress her face. "You Are Home."

"This is my Home?" Celsa looks around. "Really?"

"Here. Now, do you feel loved?"

Celsa nods.

"So it is." I plant a kiss on her cheek. "So it is, my love."

I turn around to check on the others. In a blink, you are all awake, sitting in silence.

"Are you ready to head off to our next doorway?" I ask them as I walk toward the next doorway.

"Yes I AM!"

"Yes I AMMM!"

"Yes I AMMMMM!"...

"It sounds like they all are." I whisper. Next to the doorway I see Aphrodite standing there waiting. She holds the essence of the Divine Alchemy. I walk up to her and hold her hands. I open the sixth doorway, which is pastel pink—the sixth ray of the Majestic Rainbow. As the door opens, the roseate pink light spangles all around us. The sound of a harp ignites the magic in the air. Humming bees are flying everywhere.

Aphrodite leads the way in, saying, "Welcome to your Manifestation."

"This smells like MY favorite potion—The Majestic Wand!" Celsa exclaims.

"It smells like the sweetest ice cream in MY world." Celeste says excitedly.

"Let me taste it." Jeff opens his mouth and slurps the air. "Yummmm," he says, "it tastes like ... petitgrain." He licks his lips. "Sweet!"

All the other children follow Jeff and give it a try.

"Mmmmmm ... sweet? This is called bitter, in my opinion." Godfrey says.

"In my opinion, this is bitter-sweet, just like cacao, just like life." I wink at Godfrey. "Jeff, can you hear me? What did I just say? Jeff!" I shout while the others are giggling.

Jeff is running toward the garden in front of us, trying to be the first one to arrive. Amira shakes her head and holds my hand. "He is just what he is."

I smile and gesture to everyone to walk toward the garden. The garden is filled with mountains of pink manuka shrubs, surrounded by bees. When we arrive, you all pick a few flowers immediately and add them to your bouquet. As I put my nose close to a flower, its sweetness reminds me of the sweetness in life. I feel like a little child once again. As I turn around, I see you all running around, playing while enjoying the heavenly scent of the manuka flowers in the air.

"Bi ... Boo! Everything turns into presents." Celeste waves her fingers toward the manuka shrubs to experiment.

I smile, "Šhhhh ... just be present here." I see Hecate, who holds the essence of the Divine labyrinth, standing at the far end of the garden, waiting for us.

"Oh, it's Hecate over there." Sofia shouts and runs over to her. You and the other children follow.

"Look. I am sure she has our gifts in her treasure box." Amira says, dancing and jumping.

All of you look into the box Hecate has just opened eagerly. Inside the box, you spot a scroll of a map and some wands with tags "Majestic Wand."

"I WANT ONE!" You look up at Hecate.

She smiles and hands the wands out to each one of you.

"Bless you, my miracle children. Now, it's your time to manifest divine miracles and live your divine dream. Here, you say Yes to life; Yes to Love, knowing that we are all interdependently one as The Love."

"What does it truly mean to live the divine dream as The Love?" Celsa asks me.

Both Hestia, who holds the essence of the Divine Elixir, and Athena, who holds the essence of the Divine Flame, walk over from behind.

"It is to Dream from Love, Create Love, and Live Love." Hestia answers.

"It is through your curiosity that you return to your original innocence once again," Athena explains.

I smile. "Your being holds immense sacred power to create divine creations, and to manifest love in duality."

"One of the keys to attaining self-realizations is YOU standing as the creator. So now, why don't you begin to experiment with love? You have the Magic." Hestia says.

While you are standing here, absorbing their wisdom in silence, both Hestia and Athena anoint you with their essences.

As you absorb their essences, you burst out in giggles. "But where is my magic?"

"You are The Magic!" I put both hands on your cheeks.

"Bi ... Boo!"

"Bi ... Boo!"

"Bi ... Boo!"

You look around, and realize everyone else is already experimenting with their Majestic Wand. Immediately, you begin to wave your wand. "Bi ... Boo!" For the first time, your flame ignites. I bend over to kiss your cheek. "You have it." You continue to experiment until you finally weave a thread of flames.

"Now, form a circle with it," I hint to you and step back.

The moment you form your circle of flames, a diamond droplet unveils at the center and its sparkles radiate across the sky. You look up to the sky in awe, your eyes rolling with tears.

I wipe your tears with my Right Hand while embracing you with my Left. "You Are the Love." I pat your back.

"Wow. Sweet!" Godfrey exclaims with tears.

All the other children follow you and create circles of flames.

Now I know it is time to step back. As I lie on the grass, watching you all create more and more diamonds, I feel my gratitude burst from within. I believe that being the witness itself is a blessing. "My loves, my children. I love you all so much ..." I murmur, my heart full of love. I feel I am floating in the middle of the constellation, where the rainbow lights are shining from all directions. Breathing in the moist grassy air, I wonder, "What AM I?"

"Children, follow me," Hecate calls out. "This way."

When I look around, you are all already at the far end near a gate with her. I catch up quickly.

"Grandma, Grandma MA. See?" Andrea points at the gate. There, waiting at the gate between the four pillars of light are Demeter, who holds the essence of the Divine Gateway; Gaia, who holds the essence of the Divine Flower; and Iris, who holds the essence of the Divine Drum. Demeter walks forward and says, "Welcome, my loves. As you walk past this gate, you can experiment and create all that you dream of."

You and the other children all yell.

"What!"

"WHHHATT?"

"WHATTTTTT!"

I remind you all with a smile, "Šhhhh ... just be present here. Just listen."

"My love, Dream your 'Once Upon A Dream,' where my dream and your dream are interdependently one." Gaia smiles at you all.

Together with my seven fellows, I form a circle, emanating the light from our hearts to you all. Then, we begin to anoint you with our essences.

"You are a manifestation of Love, a facet of the divine," Aphrodite says.

As you receive and integrate our essences, you feel your light glow within you. Your wings unfurl.

"Now, spread your wings and fly ... ." Aphrodite says.

As Demeter opens up the Divine Gateway, she says, "Welcome Home."

"Are we going Home now?" Celeste asks.

"Is this the way to my Home? Celsa asks.

Demeter smiles. "You Are Home."

"It's okay if you cannot understand it logically. Just follow me, children." I gesture to you all to walk into the gateway.

Iris begins to drum.

"Are we leaving now?" Celsa asks

Sofia frowns. "Are we done here?"

"Where are my gifts? Aren't they supposed to give us gifts?" Godfrey asks.

"They are anchored within your light body through us anointing you with our essence," I answer." Trust, my love, Trust."

"Is it true that in here we can manifest anything and everything?" Celsa asks.

"Yes. Now, Here, we can manifest anything and everything our soul envisions. The key is to be in divine alignment. Allow divine manifestation to be birthed into being through you." I gesture for you all to follow me and say goodbye to my fellows here. "Now. Here ... This way."

And within my heart I know ...

Here, you feel ...
You remember your innocence,
You connect with your curiosity,
You create manifestations from within,
You realize you are the miracle.
"Now, I know I am loved." Grandma MA whispers to herself.
"But where is my Home?" Your heart wonders ...

THE RAINBOW DOORWAY

You and the other children follow me and walk through the gate. Diamond sparkles emanating everywhere as bright white lights. With faith, you keep walking forward until you spot The Eternal Flame again. All of us are back at the waterfall.

"What!"

WHHHATT!"

"WHATTTTTT!"

"I thought we were going Home. Grandma MA ... Why are we back here again, at where we started?"

You are all surprised and emotional.

"Now, Home is wherever you feel Love as the Love, here and now," I say gently.

"WHATTTTTT? Grandma MA, I am tired. I just want to go Home. The Home you promised us at the beginning," Celsa says.

"I feel like I am going around and around and around ... AM I getting anywhere, honestly?" Godfrey asks. "Grandma MA!"

"Grandma MA! Can you please talk in a human language for ONCE? I honestly don't know where MY HOME is," Amira says.

"F. E. E. L ... Feel." I answer and walk slowly toward you and the other children in turn. I hug you tightly and kiss your forehead. As I sit down on the grass, I gesture for you and the other children to sit in a circle. "I understand. You are all yearning to go Home, just as I once felt ... I feel all of you." In silence, I look at The Eternal Flame. "What if I tell you that 'Here' and 'Now' are the lights of your Home? Home is wherever you are love and feel loved. It is just what it is. How do you feel? Honestly, I can tell you everything I know, all the divine miracles I have experienced. Yet all these knowledges and understandings would only stay in your mind. The last thing I want you to do is to chase the divine miracles I have experienced in my life, because we are all meant to experience different miracles according to our unique spiritual path." I pause and breathe, while staring at you. "I wonder if they understand. I have so much more I want to share, but ... ," I whisper to myself. "To attain self-realizations within you, I believe the best way is to walk you through this gateway of Majestic Rainbow Love. This pilgrimage aims to awaken your light, and to attain your own self-realizations as the Divine Child, instead of just spoon-feeding you my self-realizations. I believe this is the way to love you all." I take a deep breath and get up. With faith, in prayer, I stroll toward the final doorway. I pray you come along, to experience with your heart for yourself. This last doorway is open to those who are dedicated to live life for love and only love.

In front of the last doorway, Quan Yin, holding the essence of the Majestic Orchestration, is there waiting for us. "Together, we walk through the last doorway," she says.

I hold her hand and nod. Then, I open the seventh door, which is rainbow colors—the seventh ray of the majestic rainbow. I turn around and see all you seven children waiting, smiling at me. I feel like millions of butterflies are bursting out of my heart. "I AM loved," I murmur. As I open the door, the prismatic rainbow light shimmers everywhere.

Quan Yin leads the way in, saying, "Welcome to your Sacred Harmony." Being initiated into the final doorway, you feel as if you are inside a diamond matrix with no beginning and no end. Love is all you feel here.

Sofia looks around, and calls out, "Presents. Here I AM. Here I AM! Where are you?"

I take her hand to my heart. "Still ... Šhhhh ... just be present here." I smile.

Along with the sound of chimes tinkling in the breeze, you can smell the Sacred Story Potion.

"Grandma MA. Isn't this your favorite potion?" Celsa asks.

"That's MY favorite potion!" Jeff yells.

Godfrey rolls his eyes. "We All know that, Jeff."

I smile and give all of you a pat. "All is well ... ."

As we walk forward into the Matrix, a kaleidoscope of butterflies flutters around us, and rainbow-glitter fog floods in from all directions. The matrix transposes, taking everybody by surprise. Amira grabs my hand.

"All is well." I place my hand on her back to soothe her. As the fog subsides, diamond glitter flies all around.

"That's Our Home!" Sofia screams.

"We are back Home!" Amira yelled.

"There is my cup of cacao and marshmallow!" Celeste pointing to the fire pit.

"OMG, we are Home ... but WHY is everything emanating in a rainbow hue?" Celsa asks.

"How did our garden turn into a rainbow-colored garden, Grandma MA? This is magnificent." You ask.

I smile, looking into your eyes.

"Our Home has never changed. My dear, it's you who have transformed. Now you see your Home with your divine eyes." I wonder if you and the other children understand what I mean. I look at you all. You all are in awe looking around. "All is loved. All in divine timing." I murmur to myself.

At the center of our garden, all seven of my fellows are waiting for us at the fire pit—Quan Yin holding the essence of the Majestic Orchestration; St. Germain holding the essence of the Majestic Freedom; Lao Tzu holding the essence of the Majestic Wisdom; Metatron holding the essence of the Majestic Immortality; Melchizedek holding the essence of the Majestic Order; Metatron holding the essence of the Majestic Immortality; Sanat Kumara holding the essence of the Majestic Union; and Maha Chohan holding the essence of the Majestic World. They are shining their light, holding their essence within and without.

As I stroll over, Sofia asks, "So, AM I Home Now?"

"Your Home is wherever you feel loved as The Love. When all your questions dissolve into nothingness, my love, you are Home," I repeat.

"So, Grandma MA, where is YOUR Home?" You ask.

"My Home ... Is wherever I AM, I AM I ... ."

You look at me and nod. "I know you might not fully understand this now, but one day you will," I say.

As I walk, Andrea grabs my hand and asks gently, "Grandma MA, is what we have just experienced real?"

I turn and hold both of his hands and gaze into his eyes. "Andrea, my love. The truth always lies within your heart. You must find your own answer by going within." I caress his face. "But my truth is, everything you have just experienced is real. Everything you experience within your heart is real. This is my truth."

We arrive at the fire pit, and you all sit around it. Maha Chohan walks over to me. Forehead to forehead, we gaze into each other's eyes, tears rolling down our faces. Heart to heart, we communicate beyond words. In stillness, we understand each other through our light language of love. I nod and smile. He stands beside me and holds my Right Hand. I take a deep breath in, face the fire pit, and I blow it out to all seven directions. I close my eyes and raise my Left Hand. Now, I invoke:

> "I now invoke The Eternal Flame within me,
> Pink, purple, orange, yellow, green, and blue.
> The Love, The Light, The Life.
> I AM, I AM,
> I AM I."

All of you are looking at me, being present here with me. When I open my eyes again, The Eternal Flame is ignited at the center. Staring at the flame, I AM out of words. Maha Chohan steps in to explain: "Soaking in The Eternal Flame helps to harmonize our being and return us to our original innocence through the Divine Union, to reclaim our sovereignty from our Right Hand and our Left Hand."

You are all looking at your hands, clueless.

Andrea giggles. "How about my Right Hand?"

"Put my Right Hand down, Lift my Left Hand up. Up-Down, Up-Down, I shake, I turn, I Shake, I turn around and around. Hahaha," Jeff sings.

"Šhhh ... Jeff! Just be present here ... ," Sofia says.

Maha Chohan turns to me with a smile.

"The most significant difference between wisdom learned outside of yourself and derived through self-realizations," I say, "is ... through your self-realizations, you reclaim your ability to activate your rainbow diamond light which leads to transformations in your reality automatically."

My fellows all nod with a smile.

In silence, I close my eyes and take a deep breath. Before I can breathe out, you and the children bombard me with questions.

"Grandma MA, what are all these doorways for?"

"Grandma MA, do I need to go back there?"

"Grandma MA, what else can I do there?"

"Grandma MA, what else is there?"

"Grandma MA, are there more presents for us there?"

"Grandma MA, how can I go back there?"

"Grandma MA, are your fellows all my friends, too?"

I sit down slowly in the middle of you all next to the flame. "So now, children, let me ask you ... What are all these doorways for?"

"I Don't Know ... ," you all answer in unison.

"Do you need to go back to all the doorways?"

"I Don't Know ..."

"What else can you do there?"

"I Don't Know ..."

"What else is there?"

"I Don't Know ..."

"Are there more presents for you there?"

"I Don't Know ..."

"How can you go back there?"

"I Don't Know ... "

"Are my fellows all your friends, too?"

"I Don't Know ... "

"Yes, that's perfect. The perfect reason to begin your exploration now."

"I Don't Know is the eternal key to experience this divine world of love, and the key to embodying who you really are. Now, you as the Divine Child can continue to explore, experience, experiment, and expedite your divinity. All shall be unveiled in divine timing in your own reality within duality."

It is crucial that you walk through the threshold of Majestic Rainbow Love and return to life as the Divine Child. When you live a life as your

Sacred Story in love and unity; you live in oneness within the duality in your reality.

"Only love exists in this Majestic Rainbow World—a world available to each one of us." Melchizedek says.

"You Are Never ALONE on this path," Lao Tzu adds.

"Here, our core is interconnected as part of a circle of love. Children, ignite your Flame to join us," St. Germain says.

Metatron waves to you and the other children, and gestures for you to walk over to him as he draws a circle in the air and it transforms into a matrix made out of squares, numbers and a question mark in the middle of the matrix. "Come here, my children," he says. "Have you tried playing with this?"

"I remember Grandma MA sometimes creates a matrix and tells us to put our hands on it," Andrea says.

"Oh. I remember that too. But I have no idea what it is, BUT I can certainly feel the energies of it activating in me once I place my hand on it." Celeste adds.

Metatron smiles. "So, now, just put one hand on it again."

Jeff laughs. "Left or Right?"

Metatron caresses Jeff's face. "Experiment with it."

"Not Again!" Jeff walks over and puts his Left Hand there.

Everyone looks at Jeff.

"What do you feel?" Celsa asks, curious.

Jeff giggles. "Oh well, you already know ... energy."

"Šhhhh ... just be present here," I say.

You walk up to Metatron and put your Right Hand on it.

"Oh my God." you scream, "The energy just shot straight into my heart. I am feeling dizzy. Am I going to faint? Grandma MA."

I walk over and look into your eyes. "All is well, my love. It is just another initiation." I smile and take out the Sacred Story potion. As I anoint you with it, I count, "One, two, three, four, five, six ... eleven. Done"

"Eleven? It should be Seven? Grandma MA, we all know how to count by now." Amira says.

"Yes, my love, this is MY way of counting whenever I anoint you."

"What!"

"WHATTTT?"

"WHHHHATTTTT!" Jeff laughs. "Hahaha ... YOU are so funny."

"Why? I don't get it, Grandma MA," Sofia says.

So, while handing out my set of The Creator's Potions to each one of you children, I explain. "Number 11 is a symbol of Divine Union. Number 7 represents the completion of divine creation. This is my prayer to your union as the Divine Child, by me invoking 11 on my count of 7 ... Now, you can glimpse into my magic—the logical, non-linear way of living."

As I lay you down, Melchizedek speaks, looking at the children. "Remember, my children. You are a creator. It is your divine sovereignty right."

"You are The Love through you living as the Divine Child," says St. Germain.

"You are The Star through your existence as a light being," Lao Tzu adds.

"You are The Creator through you weave all parts of yourself into wholeness," Metatron says.

"You are The Light through your divine presence," Sanat Kumara says.

"You are who you are, perfect just the way you are," I add.

Now, Maha Choha walks into the center of The Eternal Flame, pulling me along. He holds up his treasure box and opens it. Two rainbow swans soar out, flapping their translucent wings, sprinkling diamonds everywhere. He says, "Here I AM." He gestures for me to take out my own treasure box while wrapping his arm around me.

I know neither you nor other children can fully understand what this means to me as a light being. But your witnessing matters to me deeply. I take a deep breath. My eyes well up with tears; my legs tremble; my arms shake; my heart beats, flooding with feelings. 'Here I AM,' I say. I open my treasure box to share my essence for the first time, not knowing what to expect. A rainbow-colored fog gushes out. I can hear only my heartbeat. I hold my breath and wait. As the fog clears, I see a rainbow globe rising from the treasure box. "Awe ... ." I feel relieved. I hold the globe in my hands and blow on it. It bursts. Thousands of specks of rainbow-diamond dust fly across the sky. I put on my biggest smile. I look at Maha Chohan, place my head on his shoulder, sobbing in bliss. Hugging him, I whisper, "I did it."

Maha Chohan caresses my face. "Yes, my love, you did it."

I stand there, holding my essence. I slowly take out copies of my sacred scrolls—The Š, and hand it over to each one of you.

"Finally. When I hand over this sacred scroll to you, you are free to JUST BE who you are meant to be. Go wherever you are meant to go."

You all bombard me with questions:

"WHAT!"

"What do you mean? Grandma MA?"

"I Don't Know, I Don't Know, I Don't Know ... ."

"Are you leaving us?"

"I Don't Know, I Don't Know, I Don't Know ... ."

"What are we supposed to do without you?"

"I Don't Know. Perhaps, your answer is in The Š?"

"Seriously?"

"I Don't Know, I Don't Know, I Don't Know ... ."

GRANDMA MA, What Do YOU Actually KNOW!

"Following My Love, I know. The Love, I know."

"I LOVE YOU ALL, and THIS I know. My Love, I will see you whenever I am meant to." Tears are running down my face.

"But NO, Grandma MA, NOOooooo!" Jeff places his head in his hands and sobs.

"Just say YESSSSSSSSSSSsssssssssssssssss to Love!" I cry.

Now, all my children cry, "But ... I Don't Know, I Don't Know, I Don't Know ... ."

With tears all over my face, I hold up my wand and do according to what I know. "Bi ... Boo! Šhhhh ... just be present here," I remind you all. In a blink, all your carriages filled with hydrangeas arrive at end of the Divine Aisle. I paint a rainbow circle around you and the other children seven times. Then I cloak each of you with a facet of the "Š Diamond." In silence, forehead to forehead, I place my love in you. Then I weave an arch of diamonds into your bouquet as the final touch. "Like a spoonful of sugar, transforming all sufferings into love!" I smile and look at all of you. I wave my wand "Bi ... Boo!" In silence, The Divine Aisle appears next to the well. I lead the way over to the aisle, witnessing you holding your flower bouquets as the brides of Love. One by one, you walk down the aisle. The sacred breeze, layer by layer, strips you down until only innocence and curiosity are left in your heart. You step onto your carriage, leaving behind all your old stories.

Together with my forty-nine fellows, we witness you stepping into your divine carriages while upholding your iridescence rainbow lights, just like the rest of us here. We wave and sing the song—"*We Are Home*":

"The Rainbow is shining, flowing, and birthing through us all,
As I celebrate you, you celebrate me.
We live, we live in sacred harmony.
The Rainbow is shining, flowing, and birthing through us all,
Om MA, Om MA, Om MA, Om Ma, Om MA
Om Mani Padme Hum, Om Mani Padme Hum, Om Mani Padme Hum,
Om Mani Padme Hum, Om Mani Padme Hum. Om Mani Padme Hum,
Om MA, Om MA, Om MA, Om MA, Om MA
We are light; We are compassion; We are forgiveness;
We are acceptance; We are whole; We are one.
Om MA, Om MA, Om MA, Om MA, Om MA ... ."

As we sing, we witness you all dissolving into the iridescent lights, where the Divine Prism resides. I cry blissful tears. I know you are now here with The Love; in Love; and Loved. You are Home.

And within my heart I know ...

Here, you feel ...
You remember your Divine Child,
You connect with your rainbow diamond light,
You create your Sacred Story from within,
You realize you are the harmony.
"Now, I know I am loved." Grandma MA whispers to herself.
"Now I know I AM love, Now I know I AM Home." Your heart realizes ...

Now, your heart whispers ...

Where AM I?

I Don't Know, I Don't Know, I Don't Know ...

What AM I?

I Don't Know, I Don't Know, I Don't Know ...

Who AM I?

I Don't Know, I Don't Know, I Don't Know ...

"Once upon a time, I dreamed that one day I would live in a rainbow world of love and unity."

As you comprehend The Second Movement, you walk through your second rite of passage to return as the Divine Child just the way you are. Now, I am one step closer to my dream because of you.

My beloved children, leave your questions here.

From nothingness, you continue your sacred initiation now.

Once upon a time, I dreamed that one day I would live in a rainbow
world of love and unity.

As you complete this transformation... I was brought out...
shoulder... pessimistic...such as having... the way you are.
Now I am not sure... because... you...

the following... take you... your decisions here

From now on, you'll control your actions and/or now

THIRD Š MOVEMENT

THE REBIRTH THROUGH
EXPERIMENTS

8	77	22	4	22	77	8
7	3	11	6	11	3	7
66	88	2	5	2	88	66
9	33	1	?	1	33	9
66	88	2	5	2	88	66
7	3	11	6	11	3	7
8	77	22	4	22	77	8

"The Experiments"

*Place your left hand on the square to begin your Third Rite of Passage. Allow the energy to activate your light body.

WHO AM I?
Is This A Question?
Is This Not A Question?

THE Š DOCTRINE

To return as the Divine Child, we must:

Remember the nature of the Divine Child;
Connect with the soul of the Divine Child;
Create from the heart of the Divine Child;
Live out the dream of the Divine Child.

To Begin your Sacred Initiation, it takes one thought to say ...
"YES"

—

Yes to The Love,
Yes to The Light,
Yes to The Life

!

My beloved children,

Finally, the time has come. I can now hand over to you the sacred scroll of Majestic Rainbow Love—The Š, because you have walked through all its seven doorways. The Š is a philosophical way of sacred living derived from my communion with the Divine. It aims to assist us, as humankind, in reclaiming our full sovereignty, and returning to life as a facet of the Divine—The Divine Child. I have always wanted to share with you The Š, but this can only occur under the divine order in divine timing. When you finally begin to read The Š, I may or may not be around you. I Don't Know. Either way, the truth is, we are eternally connected at our core; we are one as The Love.

The Š is sectioned into four passages:
- The Š Doctrine,
- The Š Bell,
- The Š Matrix,
- The Š Testimony.

The sound of Š—"sh" is the Key to dropping your mind into your heart. When the Heart-Mind union takes place, your return as the Divine Child begins. There are infinite pathways you, as The Love, can create from The Š. Through your intuition, you can create your unique pathway to your Divine Union. As you walk your full-circle life in alignment; live out your dreams in Divine Union; and leave behind your Sacred Story on Earth in the name of Love, you ascend by virtue of your descent in life. Šhhhh ...

Grandma M.A.

"We—The Divine Child."

The Majestic Rainbow Orchestration

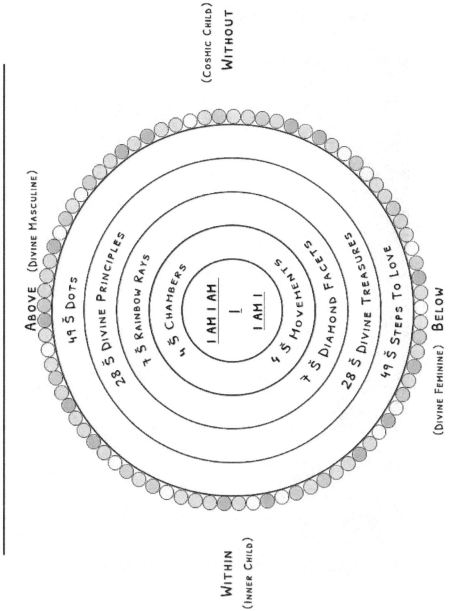

Above (Divine Masculine)

(Cosmic Child)
Without

(Divine Feminine) Below

Within
(Inner Child)

49 Š Dots
28 Š Divine Principles
7 Š Rainbow Rays
4 Š Chambers

I AM I AM
I
I AM I

4 Š Movements
7 Š Diamond Facets
28 Š Divine Treasures
49 Š Steps To Love

The Majestic Rainbow Orchestration

The Majestic Rainbow Orchestration is a cosmic matrix. It provides you with an overview of The Š—a philosophical a way of sacred living that you can live by as the Divine Child. This system is comprised of four divisions—The 4 Š strands, as its configuration. Within it, The Majestic Rainbow Orchestration comprises four layers:

1. The 4 Š Chambers, and The 4 Š Movements.
2. The 7 Š Rainbow Rays, and The 7 Š Diamond Facets.
3. The 28 Š Divine Principles, and The 28 Š Divine Treasures.
4. The 49 Š Dots, and The 49 Š Steps To Love.

By weaving the layers of the "Orchestration," you build a foundation in life in which you can live in your natural state—The Divine Child. It is in this state, you reclaim your throne to Co-create United Eternal Sanctuary (CUES) side by side with other ascended beings.

Within The CUES are the four cues. These are hints to show you how to weave your own "Orchestration" alive, that re-activates your rainbow diamond light. This orchestration is the hub representing the vision of Majestic Rainbow Love and the mission of The Š.

THE CUES

CUE 1

Remember The 49 Š Dots by you re-embodying the 49 Š Steps to Love.

*Hint: Be in Divine Union by you being present with your lateral thinking.

CUE 2

Reconnect with The 28 Š Divine Principles to rebirth with The 28 Š Divine Treasures in you.

*Hint: Be Creative by you being devoted to your imagination.

CUES 3

Rebirth through The 7 Š Rainbow Rays by you reconnecting with The 7 Š Diamond Facets.

*Hint: Reconnect with the eternal love by you accepting your conscious intuitive logic.

CUES 4

Re-embody The 4 Š Chambers as the Divine Child by you remembering The 4 Š Movements.

*Hint: Remember that you are the sanctuary by you being honest with your feelings.

THE 4 Š STRANDS

WHITE STRAND
Above

The Key: To Love

(DIVINE MASCULINE)

GREEN STRAND
Within

The Key: To Heal

(INNER CHILD)

BLACK STRAND
Below

The Key: To Create

(DIVINE FEMININE)

PINK STRAND
Without

The Key: To Just Be

(COSMIC CHILD)

THE 4 Š CHAMBERS

THE CONSORT
Exabit

Divine Essences

THE ALCHEMIST
Exabit

Divine Senses

THE CREATOR
Exabit

Divine Presences

THE COSMIC CHILD
Exabit

Divine Wisdoms

THE 4 Š MOVEMENTS

First Š Movement
The Remembrance
of Divine Union
through Exploration

Second Š Movement
The Reconnection
with your Spirit
through Experiences

Third Š Movement
The Rebirth
of our Being
through Experiments

Fourth Š Movement
The Re-embodiment
as the Divine Child
through Expedition

THE 4 Š STRANDS

The 4 Š Strands comprise the configuration of your light body, and represent your natural state of being: The Divine Child. These four-vibrational strands make up the backbone of your light body. They intertwine and create the energetic and physical structure within your being. These strands also represent the four directions of the cosmos: Above, Below, Within, and Without. Each direction signifies a correspondingly divine aspect within us:

+ The Divine Masculine,
+ The Inner Child,
+ The Divine Feminine, and
+ The Cosmic Child.

By weaving these strands together, your rainbow diamond light, representing your Divine Union, is reactivated. Thus, your Majestic Rainbow Orchestration comes alive; You reawaken your understanding of your own divinity. This leads you to your re-embodiment as the Divine Child, which enables you to "Co-Create United Eternal Sanctuary" as a selfless service with other ascended beings, fulfilling the next phase of the Divine's dream at the dawn of time: to live in love and unity with all creations in your reality. Life becomes your playground.

WHITE STRAND: Represents The Above.

Divine Aspect: Divine Masculine.
The Key: To Love.

GREEN STRAND: Represents The Within.

> **Divine Aspect:** Inner Child.
> **The Key:** To Heal.

BLACK STRAND: Represents The Below.

> **Divine Aspect:** Divine Feminine.
> **The Key:** To Create.

PINK STRAND: Represents The Without.

> **Divine Aspect:** Cosmic Child.
> **The Key:** To Just Be.

The 4 Š Chambers

The 4 Š Chambers are four core archetypes of your divinity:

+ Consort's Chamber,
+ Alchemist's Chamber,
+ Creator's Chamber, and
+ Cosmic Child's Chamber.

Each of the chambers holds and exhibits a unique quality. These qualities are your four keys to understand your divinity: Divine Essence, Divine Senses, Divine Presence, Divine Wisdom. Human beings tend to focus on embodying one chamber at a time, but there are no rules as to how to navigate amongst the 4 Š Chambers to create inner balance. When you re-embody all 4 Š Chambers, you experience wholeness as the Divine Child.

Consort's Chamber

When you re-embody this chamber, you become a Divine Lover; a lover in alignment with your own soul and in Divine Union with all of creations. You Here, you understand and exhibit the Divine Essence within you.

ALCHEMIST'S CHAMBER

When you re-embody this chamber, you activate all divine alchemical gifts within and without. These alchemical gifts enable you to weave your spirit into wholeness through energy frequencies. Here, you understand and exhibit the Divine Senses within you.

CREATOR'S CHAMBER

When you re-embody this chamber, you activate your inner birthing portal. This enables you to give birth to both tangible and intangible matters and rebirth yourself as the Divine Child. You become the Divine Creator, creating directly from The Void of nothingness. Here, you understand and exhibit the Divine Presence within you.

COSMIC CHILD'S CHAMBER

When you re-embody this chamber, you experience your original innocence. This enables you to surrender and accept all human emotions that arise from within you. This Chamber is located at the core of your being. Here, you begin to re-embody as the Divine Child and attain self-realizations. Thus, you exhibit the Divine Wisdom within you.

THE 4 Š MOVEMENTS

The 4 Š Movements are the four seasons of the divine life on earth. The four seasons represent your process to remember, reconnect, rebirth, and re-embody your divinity. Each season is a rotation of cyclical initiation, perpetually in motion. Therefore, in your life, you move in a non-linear way through all four of them at the macro and micro level. Flowing consciously among the 4 Š Movements daily supports you in fine-tuning your inner balance, which empowers you to explore, experience, experiment, and expedite your ascension.

THE FIRST Š MOVEMENT
The Remembrance of Soul Union through explorations.

It is through exploration of innocence that you remember your soul. Thus, you open up the sacred heart portal within you to live life in Divine Union.

THE SECOND Š MOVEMENT
The Reconnection with your Spirit through experiences.

It is through experiencing life in innocence that you reconnect with your spirit. As the result, you weave all aspects of yourself into one and experience wholeness from within you.

THE THIRD Š MOVEMENT
The Rebirth of your being through experiments.

It is through experimenting in life in innocence that you, step-by-step expand your rainbow diamond light body. When you give birth to divine creations and rebirth your own being into unity with the Divine, you attain self-realizations and gain divine wisdom through this process. Here, you experience divine miracles and understand its magnificents.

THE FOURTH Š MOVEMENT
The Re-embodiment as the Divine Child through expeditions.

It is through your life's expedition that you unite and re-embody your core divine aspects—the Divine Masculine, Inner Child, Divine Feminine, and Cosmic Child. As a result, you return to life as the Divine Child. Thus, you reach ascension through your whole being descending to life in this state. You live your highest potential available for humankind.

THE 7 Š RAINBOW RAYS

1st Ray

2nd Ray

3rd Ray

4th Ray

5th Ray

6th Ray

7th Ray

THE 7 Š RAINBOW RAYS

The 7 Š Rainbow Rays are the seven main frequencies embedded in the core of all divine creations that are birthed from the Divine Prism. Just like any divine creation, when we, humankind are birthed from the Divine Prism, we are automatically implanted with these rays. This is a divine alchemical process, transforming energy vibrations into tangible physical matter on earth. When you reconnect with The 7 Š Rainbow Rays, you reawaken your understanding of yourself as the Creator. Hence, you re-claim your alchemical ability to birth divine creations into physicality, in the same alchemical process you were birthed in. Furthermore, you also reactivate your innate ability to rebirth yourself into wholeness.

✦ FIRST Š RAINBOW RAY – Pastel Purple. ♥

✦ SECOND Š RAINBOW RAY – Pastel Blue. ♥

✦ THIRD Š RAINBOW RAY – Pastel Green. ♥

✦ FOURTH Š RAINBOW RAY – Pastel Yellow.

✦ FIFTH Š RAINBOW RAY – Pastel Orange. ♥

✦ SIXTH Š RAINBOW RAY – Pastel Pink. ♥

✦ SEVENTH Š RAINBOW RAY – Pastel Rainbow. ♥ ♥ ♥ ♥ ♥

THE ✝ Š DIAMOND FACET

Venetian Facet
Traits: Rose, Lotus-Rose, The Mother, The Goddess, Infinite Love.

Celtic Facet
Traits: Mushroom, Moon, The Fairy, The Mystics, Infinite Healing.

Indian Facet
Traits: Spices, Star, The Yogi, The Seeress, Infinite Wisdom.

Egyptian Facet
Traits: Frankincense, Gold, The Minister, The Alchemist, Infinite Will.

Nordic Facet
Traits: Pine cones, Sun, The Musician, The Herbalist, Infinite Humility.

Hellenism Facet
Traits: Olives, Pearl, The Artist, The Enchantress, Infinite Manifestation.

Cosmic Facet
Traits: Crystals, Diamond, The Philosopher, The Sage, Infinite Harmony.

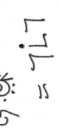

The 7 Š Diamond Facets

The 7 Š Diamond Facets represents the seven core divine traits within your whole being. Each facet also represents as a universal lineage you can identify with in the world. Each of you encompass all seven facets within you. While some traits are obvious, some are hidden. When you reconnect with The 7 Š Diamond Facets, your expansion of consciousness fine-tunes your inner balance and deepens your understanding of the make up of your divinity.

Venetian Facet ♥
Represents the essence of the Mother.

 ✦ **Traits:** Rose, Lotus-Rose, The Mother, The Goddess, Infinite Love.
 "Now, as the Mother, you represent the vibration of infinite love on earth."

Celtic Facet ♥
Represents the essence of the Maiden.

 ✦ **Traits:** Mushroom, Moon, The Fairy, The Mystics, Infinite Healing.
 "Now, as the Maiden, you represent the vibration of infinite healing on earth."

INDIAN FACET ♥
Represents the essence of the Wise Women.

✦ Traits: Spices, Star, The Yogi, The Seeress, Infinite Wisdom.
"Now, as the Wise Woman, you represent the vibration of infinite wisdom on earth."

EGYPTIAN FACET
Represents the essence of the Mystic.

✦ Traits: Frankincense, Gold, The Minister, The Alchemist, Infinite Will.
"Now, as the Mystic, you represent the vibration of infinite will on earth."

NORDIC FACET ♥
Represents the essence of the Wisdom Keeper.

✦ Traits: Pine Cones, Sun, The Musician, The Herbalist, Infinite Humility.
"Now, as the Wisdom Keeper, you represent the vibration of infinite humility on earth."

HELLENISM FACET ♥
Represents the essence of the Newborn.

✦ Traits: Olives, Pearl, The Artist, The Enchantress, Infinite Manifestation.
"Now, as the Newborn, you represent the vibration of infinite manifestation on earth."

COSMIC FACET ♥ ♥ ♥   ♥ ♥
Represents the essence of the Cosmic Child.

✦ Traits: Crystals, Diamond, The Philosopher, The Sage, Infinite Harmony.
"Now, as The Cosmic Child, you represent the vibration of infinite harmony on earth."

THE 28 Š DIVINE PRINCIPLES

	White Pillar	Green Pillar	Black Pillar	Pink Pillar
Venetian Facet	1 Eternal Love	14 Know	15 Perform	28 Perform The Divine Play
Celtic Facet	2 Innate Healing	13 See	16 Vulnerableness	27 Embrace our vulnerableness
Indian Facet	3 Gnosis Wisdom	12 Hear	17 Birth	26 Birth Divine Creations
Egyptian Facet	4 Divine Will	11 Smell	18 Witness	25 Witness The Eternal Flame
Nordic Facet	5 Humility	10 Taste	19 Devote	24 Flow With Devotion
Hellenism Facet	6 Manifestation	9 Feel	20 Unite	23 Live Union In Duality
Cosmic Facet	7 Sascred Harmony	8 Touch	21 Just Be	22 Be The Divine Child

THE 28 Š DIVINE PRINCIPLES

The 28 Š Divine Principles are the macro precepts to uphold. Each principle should be defined within you through your communion with the Divine. The process of forming your own perceptions of these principles helps you reclaim and live in your full sovereignty. Your comprehension of these principles becomes the reference point that supports you, refines your inner balance, and sustains your divine alignment at all levels as the Divine Child. Hence, you reawaken your understanding of yourself as the Alchemist.

The 28 Š Divine Principles are categorized into four main categories:
+ **Divine Essence**: represented by The Consort.
+ **Divine Senses**: represented by The Alchemist.
+ **Divine Presence**: represented by The Creator.
+ **Divine Wisdom**: represented by The Cosmic Child.

The Consort holds Divine Principles Nos. 1-7, which are the Divine Essence. As you uphold these principles, you exhibit all Divine Essence within you. The Š Divine Principles includes:

1. Eternal Love.
2. Innate Healing.
3. Gnosis Wisdom.
4. Divine Will.
5. Humility.
6. Manifestation.
7. Sacred Harmony.

The Alchemist holds the Divine Principles Nos. 8-14, which are the Divine Senses. As you uphold these principles, you reactivate all your Divine Senses within you. The Š Divine Principles includes:

8. Touch.
9. Feel.
10. Taste.
11. Smell.
12. Hear.
13. See.
14. Know.

The Creator holds the Divine Principles Nos. 15-21, which are the Divine Presence. As you uphold these principles, you walk through life with all your Divine Presence within you. The Š Divine Principles includes:

15. Perform.
16. Vulnerableness
17. Birth.
18. Witness.
19. Devote.
20. Unite.
21. Just Be.

The Cosmic Child holds Divine Principles Nos. 22-28, which are the Divine Wisdom. As you uphold these principles, you live life with all your Divine Wisdom within you. The Š Divine Principles includes:

22. Be the Divine Child.
23. Live union in duality.
24. Flow in life with devotion.
25. Witness The Eternal Flame.
26. Birth divine creations.
27. Embrace our vulnerableness.
28. Perform the divine play.

THE 28 Š DIVINE TREASURES

	White Pillar	Green Pillar	Black Pillar	Pink Pillar
Venetian Facet	1 Sacred Heart	14 Whole-Being	15 Divine Scroll	28 Sacred Harmony
Celtic Facet	2 Enchanted Cauldron	13 Yin Yang Balance	16 Divine Marriage	27 Manifestation
Indian Facet	3 All Seein-Eye	12 Blood	17 The Creator's Bowl	26 Humility
Egyptian Facet	4 Immortal Candle	11 Chi	18 The Eternal Flame	25 Divine Will
Nordic Facet	5 Infinite Light	10 Five Elements	19 Channel of Light	24 Gnosis Wisdom
Hellenism Facet	6 Majestic Wand	9 Digestion	20 Infinite Life Force	23 Enchanted Cauldron
Cosmic Facet	7 Sacred Story	8 Immunity	21 Sacred Vocation	22 Eternal Love

THE 28 Š DIVINE TREASURES

The 28 Š Divine Treasures are innate qualities and gifts you reclaim as you uphold the Š Divine Principles. The 28 Š Divine Treasures are instruments categorized to serve four purposes: remember your Soul, reconnect with your spirit, rebirth yourself into wholeness, re-embody as the Divine Child. Each of the 28 treasures is equally important and distinctive. Through utilizing these treasures, you reach your Divine Union and reclaim your sovereignty to write your Sacred Story in life as an eternal gift shared with our humanity.

The Consort possesses seven of The Š Divine Treasures that support you to remember your soul:
+ Divine Treasures: Sacred Heart, Enchanted Cauldron, All Seeing-Eye, Immortal Candle, Infinite Light, Majestic Wand, Sacred Story.

The Alchemist possesses seven of The Š Divine Treasures that support you to reconnect with your spirit:
+ Divine Treasures: Immunity, Digestion, Five Elements, Chi, Blood, Yin Yang Balance, Whole-Being.

The Creator possesses seven of The Š Divine Treasures that support you to rebirth into wholeness:
+ Divine Treasures: Divine Scroll, Divine Marriage, The Creator's Bowl, The Eternal Flame, Channel of Light, Infinite Life Force, Sacred Vocation.

The Cosmic Child possesses seven of The Š Divine Treasures that support you to re-embody as the Divine Child:
+ Divine Treasures: Eternal Love, Enchanted Cauldron, Gnosis Wisdom, Divine Will, Humility, Manifestation, Sacred Harmony.

THE 49 Š DOTS

	Eternal Love	Eternal Passion	Eternal Divinity	Eternal Pearl	Eternal Memoir	Eternal Remembrance	Eternal Conception
Venetian Facet	Eternal Love	Eternal Passion	Eternal Divinity	Eternal Pearl	Eternal Memoir	Eternal Remembrance	Eternal Conception
Celtic Facet	Sacred Crib	Sacred Balm	Sacred Chalice	Sacred Well	Sacred Cloak	Sacred Fountain	Sacred Key
Inidan Facet	Magnificent Egg	Magnificent Prisim	Magnificent Crown	Magnificent Chamber	Magnificent Bell	Magnificent Lamp	Magnificent Feather
Egyptian Facet	Immortal Seal	Immortal Womb	Immortal Thread	Immortal Charm	Immortal Wings	Immortal Halo	Immortal Scepter
Nordic Facet	Benevolent Star	Benevolent Realm	Benevolent Ark	Benevolent Float	Benevolent Balloon	Benevolent Arrow	Benevolent Carousel
Hellenism Facet	Divine Alchemy	Divine Elixir	Divine Flame	Divine Labyrinth	Divine Gateway	Divine Flower	Divine Drum
Cosmic Facet	Majestic Orchestration	Majestic Freedom	Majestic Wisdom	Majestic Immortality	Majestic Order	Majestic Union	Majestic World

THE 49 Š DOTS

The 49 Š Dots are ciphers inscribed in "Dots," These dots serve as transmitters, which reactivate the forty-nine essences within your soul. When you retrieve and reconnect all the Š Dots within you, you reawaken your understanding of yourself as the Consort, which leads you to experience your Divine Union. These Š Dots are also the musical "notes" of your soul song. Your soul song is an energy vibration in and around you that enables you to communicate and understand the divine beyond your logical mind. Therefore, as you reactivate the 49 Š Dots, you reclaim your innate ability to transmit Divine Love and leave its imprint on all you create and touch. This sets out your momentum to Co-create United Eternal Sanctuary (CUES).

Š DOT 1 ♥

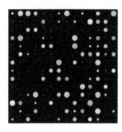

The Essence: Eternal Love

Universal Archetype: Lady Mary

Lineage: Venetian

Š DOT 2 ♥

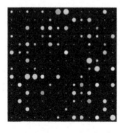

The Essence: Eternal Passion

Universal Archetype: Mary Magdalene

Lineage: Venetian

Š DOT 3 ♥

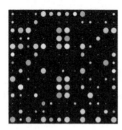

The Essence: Eternal Divinity

Universal Archetype: Green Tara

Lineage: Venetian

Š DOT 4 ♥

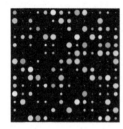

The Essence: Eternal Pearl

Universal Archetype: Black Madonna

Lineage: Venetian

Š DOT 5 ♥

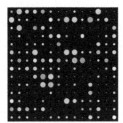

The Essence: Eternal Memoir

Universal Archetype: Lady Fatima

Lineage: Venetian

Š DOT 6 ♥

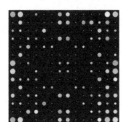

The Essence: Eternal Remembrance

Universal Archetype: Lady Nada

Lineage: Venetian

Š DOT 7 ♥

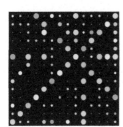

The Essence: Eternal Conception

Universal Archetype: White Tara

Lineage: Venetian

Š DOT 8 ♥

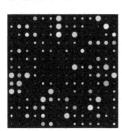

The Essence: Sacred Crib

Universal Archetype: Aine

Lineage: Celtics

Š DOT 9 ♥

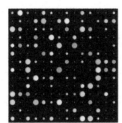

The Essence: Sacred Balm

Universal Archetype: Airmed

Lineage: Celtics

Š DOT 10 ♥

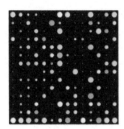

The Essence: Sacred Chalice

Universal Archetype: Danu

Lineage: Celtics

Š DOT 11 ♥

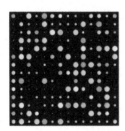

The Essence: Sacred Well

Universal Archetype: Ceridwen

Lineage: Celtics

Š DOT 12 ♥

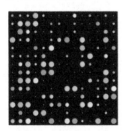

The Essence: Sacred Cloak

Universal Archetype: Olwen

Lineage: Celtics

Š DOT 13 ♥

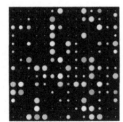

The Essence: Sacred Fountain
Universal Archetype: Rhiannon
Lineage: Celtics ♥

Š DOT 14 ♥

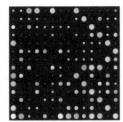

The Essence: Sacred Key
Universal Archetype: Brigid
Lineage: Celtics

Š DOT 15 ♥

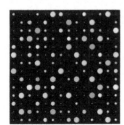

The Essence: Magnificent Egg
Universal Archetype: Rati
Lineage: Indian

Š DOT 16 ♥

The Essence: Magnificent Prism
Universal Archetype: Parvati
Lineage: Indian

Š DOT 17 ♥

The Essence: Magnificent Crown
Universal Archetype: Saraswati
Lineage: Indian

Š DOT 18 ♥

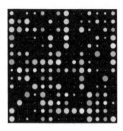

The Essence: Magnificent Chamber
Universal Archetype: Kali
Lineage: Indian

Š DOT 19 ♥

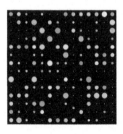

The Essence: Magnificent Bell
Universal Archetype: Aditi
Lineage: Indian

Š DOT 20 ♥

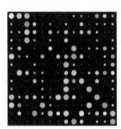

The Essence: Magnificent Lamp
Universal Archetype: Lakshmi
Lineage: Indian

Š DOT 21 ♥

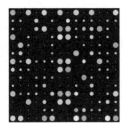

The Essence: Magnificent Feather

Universal Archetype: Shakti

Lineage: Indian

Š DOT 22

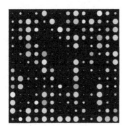

The Essence: Immortal Seal

Universal Archetype: Isis

Lineage: Egyptian

Š DOT 23

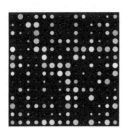

The Essence: Immortal Womb

Universal Archetype: Bastet

Lineage: Egyptian

Š DOT 24

The Essence: Immortal Thread

Universal Archetype: Hathor

Lineage: Egyptian

Š DOT 25

The Essence: Immortal Charm

Universal Archetype: Nephthys

Lineage: Egyptian

Š DOT 26

The Essence: Immortal Wings

Universal Archetype: Nut

Lineage: Egyptian

Š DOT 27

The Essence: Immortal Halo

Universal Archetype: Renenet

Lineage: Egyptian

Š DOT 28

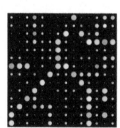

The Essence: Immortal Scepter

Universal Archetype: Maat

Lineage: Egyptian

Š DOT 29 ♥

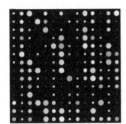

The Essence: Benevolent Star
Universal Archetype: Freya
Lineage: Nordic

Š DOT 30 ♥

The Essence: Benevolent Realm
Universal Archetype: Eir
Lineage: Nordic

Š DOT 31 ♥

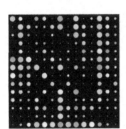

The Essence: Benevolent Ark
Universal Archetype: Snotra
Lineage: Nordic

Š DOT 32 ♥

The Essence: Benevolent Float
Universal Archetype: Hel
Lineage: Nordic

Š DOT 33 ♥

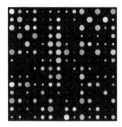

The Essence: Benevolent Balloon

Universal Archetype: Idun

Lineage: Nordic

Š DOT 34 ♥

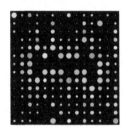

The Essence: Benevolent Arrow

Universal Archetype: Gefjun

Lineage: Nordic

Š DOT 35 ♥

The Essence: Benevolent Carousel

Universal Archetype: Sjofn

Lineage: Nordic

Š DOT 36 ♥

The Essence: Divine Alchemy

Universal Archetype: Aphrodite

Lineage: Hellenism

Š DOT 37 ♥

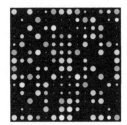

The Essence: Divine Elixir
Universal Archetype: Hestia
Lineage: Hellenism

Š DOT 38 ♥

The Essence: Divine Flame
Universal Archetype: Athena
Lineage: Hellenism

Š DOT 39 ♥

The Essence: Divine Labyrinth
Universal Archetype: Hecate
Lineage: Hellenism

Š DOT 40 ♥

The Essence: Divine Gateway
Universal Archetype: Demeter
Lineage: Hellenism

Š DOT 41 ♥

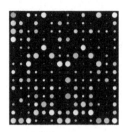

The Essence: Divine Flower

Universal Archetype: Gaia

Lineage: Hellenism

Š DOT 42 ♥

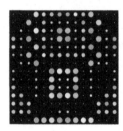

The Essence: Divine Drum

Universal Archetype: Iris

Lineage: Hellenism

Š DOT 43 ♥ ♥ ♥   ♥ ♥

The Essence: Majestic Orchestration

Universal Archetype: Quan Yin

Lineage: Cosmic

Š DOT 44 ♥ ♥ ♥   ♥ ♥

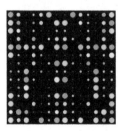

The Essence: Majestic Freedom

Universal Archetype: St. Germain

Lineage: Cosmic

Š DOT 45 ♥ ♥ ♥ ♥ ♥

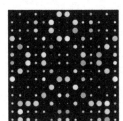

The Essence: Majestic Wisdom

Universal Archetype: Lao Tzu

Lineage: Cosmic

Š DOT 46 ♥ ♥ ♥ ♥ ♥

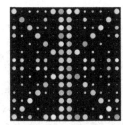

The Essence: Majestic Immortality

Universal Archetype: Metatron

Lineage: Cosmic

Š DOT 47 ♥ ♥ ♥ ♥ ♥

The Essence: Majestic Order

Universal Archetype: Melchizedek

Lineage: Cosmic

Š DOT 48 ♥ ♥ ♥ ♥ ♥

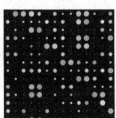

The Essence: Majestic Union

Universal Archetype: Sanat Kumara

Lineage: Cosmic

Š Dot 49 ♥ ♥ ♥ ♥ ♥

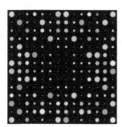

The Essence: Majestic World

Universal Archetype: Maha Chohan

Lineage: Cosmic

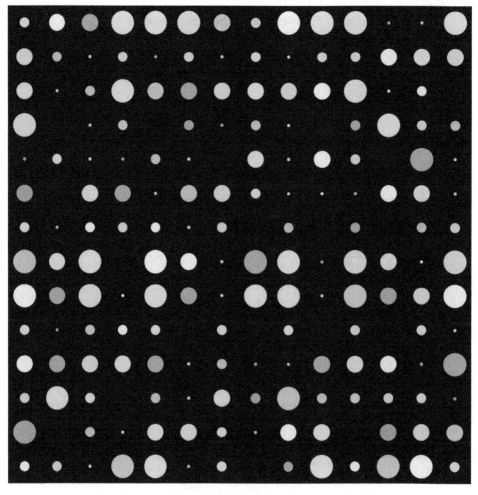

"Š Dot 0 – I AM I"

THE 49 Š STEPS TO LOVE

Venetian Facet	Once Upon A Dream	Open To Love	Naked	Dragon	Book of Love	Remembering Heart	Conceived
Celtic Facet	Hibernation	Umbrella	My Cauldron	Sanctuary	All is Well	Embrace	My Key
Indian Facet	Innate	The Eye	Majestic Clown	Mirror Mirror	Aloha	Simplicity	Rainbow Peacock
Egyptian Facet	Horn	Universal Maternity	Web of Love	Swan	Falcon	Majestic Trampoline	Triumph
Nordic Facet	Humility	Love Compass	Captin	Barrel Surfer	Circle of Life	A Juggler	Merry-Go-Round
Hellenism Facet	Bibidi Boo	Soft Power	Seven Hearts	Dandelion	Hot-Air Balloon	Blossom	Graditude
Cosmic Facet	I AM Miracle	Rainbow Unicorn	My Carriage	My Eternal Dream	The Diamond	Happy Birthday	My World

"Once upon a Dream" ≈ Dream of Earth

⊚ → ⊙ → ⊘ → Sacred Union

THE 49 Š STEPS TO LOVE

The 49 Š Steps to Love is a non-linear cosmic spiral designed as a pathway that leads you to your Divine Union; to manifeste a divine life in your reality. Your Divine Union is the foundation of your union with all creations, and the first phase of your re-embodiment as the Divine Child. These steps grant you a glimpse into the Divine's dream behind its creation of the Earth at the dawn of time—"Once Upon A Dream"—and serves as a light and an inspiration to write your Sacred Story in life.

STEP 1 ♥

ONCE UPON A DREAM

Decoding Hint: When Lotus meets The Sun.

STEP 2 ♥

OPEN TO LOVE

Decoding Hint: My passion ignites.

STEP 3 ♥

NAKED

Decoding Hint: I AM stripped.

STEP 4 ♥

DRAGON
   Decoding Hint: I tame my primordiality.

STEP 5 ♥

BOOK OF LOVE
   Decoding Hint: Love is eternal.

STEP 6 ♥

REMEMBERING HEART
   Decoding Hint: Sealed with a kiss.

STEP 7 ♥

CONCEIVED
   Decoding Hint: When three become one

STEP 8 ♥

HIBERNATION
   Decoding Hint: It's time for one and only me.

STEP 9 ♥

UMBRELLA
   Decoding Hint: I know what's best for me.

STEP 10 ♥

MY CAULDRON
   Decoding Hint: A dose of Love.

STEP 11 ♥

SANCTUARY
   Decoding Hint: I bathe.

STEP 12 ♥

ALL IS WELL
Decoding Hint: I surrender.

STEP 13 ♥

EMBRACE
Decoding Hint: I breathe.

STEP 14 ♥

MY KEY
Decoding Hint: I unlock.

STEP 15 ♥

INNATE
Decoding Hint: Love is born in me.

STEP 16 ♥

THE EYE
Decoding Hint: My vision.

STEP 17 ♥

MAJESTIC CLOWN
Decoding Hint: I see beyond the veil.

STEP 18 ♥

MIRROR MIRROR
Decoding Hint: I AM the truth.

STEP 19 ♥

ALOHA
Decoding Hint: I AM perfect just the way I AM.

STEP 20 ♥

SIMPLICITY

Decoding Hint: I AM simply magnificent.

STEP 21 ♥

RAINBOW PEACOCK

Decoding Hint: I AM the dream of my life.

STEP 22

HORN

Decoding Hint: I lift up my horn

STEP 23

UNIVERSAL MATERNITY

Decoding Hint: My innate motherhood.

STEP 24

WEB OF LOVE

Decoding Hint: I weave my dream and dance it alive.

STEP 25

SWAN

Decoding Hint: I light up the way.

STEP 26

FALCON

Decoding Hint: Ready, Get set, Go.

STEP 27

MAJESTIC TRAMPOLINE

Decoding Hint: I surpass my imagination.

STEP 28

TRIUMPH

Decoding Hint: Doors open; Path cleared.

STEP 29 ♥

HUMILITY

Decoding Hint: I AM down to earth.

STEP 30 ♥

LOVE COMPASS

Decoding Hint: I know the way.

STEP 31 ♥

CAPTAIN

Decoding Hint: I steer my wheel.

STEP 32 ♥

BARREL SURFER

Decoding Hint: I ride waves with ease.

STEP 33 ♥

CIRCLE OF LIFE

Decoding Hint: I dance; I fly; I dive.

STEP 34 ♥

A JUGGLER

Decoding Hint: My action birthed in stillness.

STEP 35 ♥

MERRY-GO-ROUND

Decoding Hint: I just play up and down.

STEP 36 ♥

BIBIDI BOO
Decoding Hint: I AM the creator of my dream.

STEP 37 ♥

SOFT POWER
Decoding Hint: Like water; like air.

STEP 38 ♥

SEVEN HEARTS
Decoding Hint: I sing my manifestation.

STEP 39 ♥

DANDELION
Decoding Hint: My wishes are answered.

STEP 40 ♥

HOT-AIR BALLOON
Decoding Hint: I AM free.

STEP 41 ♥

BLOSSOM
Decoding Hint: I witness.

STEP 42 ♥

GRATITUDE
Decoding Hint: Thank You.

STEP 43 ♥ ♥ ♥ ♥ ♥

I AM MIRACLE
Decoding Hint: Because I trust.

Step 44 ♥ ♥ ♥ ♥ ♥

Rainbow Unicorn
Decoding Hint: My dream life swirls into place.

Step 45 ♥ ♥ ♥ ♥ ♥

My Carriage
Decoding Hint: I love my present.

Step 46 ♥ ♥ ♥ ♥ ♥

My Eternal Dream
Decoding Hint: Our dreams are interdependently one.

Step 47 ♥ ♥ ♥ ♥ ♥

The Diamond
Decoding Hint: Yes, I do.

Step 48 ♥ ♥ ♥ ♥ ♥

Happy Birthday
Decoding Hint: I AM born.

Step 49 ♥ ♥ ♥ ♥ ♥

My World
Decoding Hint: I Live.

THE 28 Š BELLS

My beloved children,
Now is your time to ring the Š Bells,
To hear the voice of the Divine Child,
And begin your re-embodiment
Now

.

.

.

As you read the 28 Š Bell aloud, you ring the bell of the Divine Child metaphorically, to awaken and summon it to reunite within you. When you awaken all its facets within, you begin to hear the wisdom of the Divine Child through your own communion.

Š Bell ı

The Venetian Consort

Eternal Love is a Baby Purple.
This is the way I am loving it.

SAY
Yes, I Do

.

Just because I know I Love You.
This is all I do, even in times without a clue;
&
* NOW *
As I give my heart to everything
I KNOW
|
I am in union with my Sacred Heart.

The Divine Union,
With
I

.

.

.

Š Bell 2

The Venetian Alchemist

With divine alignment, I radiate Divine Love toward all creations;

With deep listening, I understand all visions of the divine play;

With forgiveness, I dissolve my judgments as they arise;

With humility, I flow in all the roles I choose to play;

With compassion, I fall in love with all creations;

With my sacred heart, I unleash all my love;

With acceptance, I live in peace.

* NOW *
as
I KNOW

,

I RISE

.

Š Bell 3

The Venetian Creator

Love is Love.
Jasmine Knows.

The healing love is what Ylang Ylang Knows.

Davana Knows the wisdom of love.

While the will to love is what Benzoin Knows.

Lavender Knows ...
the humility within love;
Perhaps also...the love within humility.

Niaouli Knows how to manifest Love
Here & Now.

Neroli is the one who Knows
the harmony of eternal love.
&
Ruby Just Knows
.

* NOW *

,

as
I PERFORM
...
I LIVE

.

Š Bell 4

The Venetian Child

As I walk in Nothingness,
I Now live my divinity

.

I AM ETERNAL LOVE
&
* NOW *

I AM I AM

.

I AM I

.

I
JUST BE

.

Š Bell 5

The Celtic Consort

Innate Healing is a Baby Blue.
This is the way I am loving it.

SAY
Yes, I Do
.

Just because I know I Love You.
This is all I do, even in times without a clue;
&
* NOW *
As I give my heart to everything
I SEE
|
I am in union with my Enchanted Cauldron.

The Divine Union,
With
I

.

.

.

Š Bell 6

The Celtic Alchemist

When I AM performing,
I am present in all the roles I choose to play;

When I AM authentic,
I am present to experience beyond my imagination;

When I AM empowered,
I am present in my union with all of creations;

When I AM grounded,
I am present with my gnosis-knowing within;

When I AM courageous,
I am present, living in immortal love;

When I AM passionate,
I am present at the core of my divinity;

When I AM contemplating,
I am present with the dream of the Divine.

* NOW *
as
I SEE

,

I RISE

.

Š Bell 7

The Celtic Creator

Rose
Sees
the love through healing.

And
Juniper Berry
Sees our ability to heal.

Clary Sage Sees clearly how to heal.

While Raven Sara is the one who Sees ...
The healing of divine will.

Bergamot is graceful.
It Sees the humbleness of our innate healing.

And, Cedarwood is the one who can See,

...

the manifestation of healings.

While harmony is what Patchouli Sees in healing.
&
Serpentine Just Sees.

.

* NOW *
as
I AM VULNERABLENESS

...

I LIVE

.

Š Bell 8

The Celtic Child

As I Dream,
I Now live my Sacred Story

·

I AM INNATE HEALING
&
* NOW *

I AM I AM

·

I AM I

·

I
JUST BE

·

Š Bell 9

The Indian Consort

Gnosis Wisdom is a Baby Green.
This is just the way I am loving it.

SAY
Yes, I Do
.

Just because I know I Love You.
This is all I do, even in times without a clue;
&
* NOW *
As I give my heart to everything
I HEAR
|
I am in union with my All-Seeing Eye.

The Divine Union,
With
I

.

.

.

Š Bell 10

The Indian Alchemist

As I perform in ceremonies, the truth of all creations reveal;

As I AM feeling vulnerable, duality dissolves;

As I reach self-realizations, all wisdom unveils in order;

As I breathe, gratitude bursts out in every present moment;

As I play, my being is transformed to innocence;

As I create, gnosis is reclaimed;

As I surrender
,
The Seed of Life
meets
The Egg;

* NOW *
as
I HEAR
,
I RISE
.

Š Bell II

The Indian Creator

Coriander
Hears the love within wisdom

while our healing wisdom is what Cinnamon Hears

.

.

.

The infinite spiral of wisdom is what I Hear.
Cardamom cries.

And,
as Nutmeg scries,
It Hears the wisdom of the divine will power.

Clove Bud humbly Hears...
Hearing the wisdom behind humility.

Pepper Hears...
The wisdom of manifestation

Ginger, the wisdom keeper,
Hears the wisdom of harmony
&
Shiva Lingham Just Hears

.

* NOW *
as
I BIRTH

...

I LIVE

.

Š Bell 12

The Indian Child

As I Inscribe,
I Now realize the wisdom behind all creations

·

I AM GNOSIS WISDOM
&
* NOW *

I AM I AM

·

I AM I

·

I
JUST BE

·

Š Bell 13

The Egyptian Consort

Divine Will is a Baby Yellow.
This is just the way I am loving it.

SAY
Yes, I Do

.

Just because I know I Love You.
This is all I do, even in times without a clue;
&
* NOW *
As I give my heart to everything
I SMELL
|
I am in union with my Immortal Candle.

The Divine Union,
With
I

.

.

.

Š Bell 14

The Egyptian Alchemist

I Just Perform,
And I give it all;

I Just Be Vulnerable,
And strip down passionately;

I Just Birth,
And it takes only one thought;

I Just Let Go,
And allow the love to be bestowed;

I Just Dance,
And paint it with circles of rainbows;

I Just Pray,
And it is a selfless service;

I Just Flow,
And play with the flow.

* NOW *
as
I SMELL

,

I RISE

.

Š Bell 15

The Egyptian Creator

The Sacred Frankincense
Smells
the will to love;

While its twin, Myrrh,
Smells the divine will of healing.

Smelling the wisdom within the divine will is how Cistus loves being.

Hyssop is powerful,
As it can Smell the will of divine will and heals.

The Copaiba
!
the humbleness within the divine will,
is what it Smells.

Galbanum
Smells the manifestation of the will,
So it is. So it is. So it is.

Cypress
just Smells the divine will in harmony.
&
Lapis Lazuli Just Smells

.

* NOW *
as
I WITNESS
...
I LIVE

.

Š Bell 16

The Egyptian Child

As I Reflect,
I am Now on fire

.

I AM DIVINE WILL
&
* NOW *

I AM I AM

.

I AM I

.

I
JUST BE

.

Š Bell 17

The Nordic Consort

Humility is a Baby Orange.
This is just the way I am loving it.

SAY
Yes, I Do

.

Just because I know I Love You.
This is all I do, even in times without a clue;
&
* NOW *
As I give my heart to everything
I TASTE
|
I am in union with my Infinite Light.

The Divine Union,
With
I

.

.

.

Š Bell 18

The Nordic Alchemist

I let the performance flow through me;

I let my vulnerableness to be acknowledged;

I let the birthing be part of my life;

I let my witness be a testimony;

I let grace be expressed;

I let curiosity be my guide to live by;

I let enchantments fly across the universe.

* NOW *

I Devote.
&
I Live

.

Š Bell 19

The Nordic Creator

Fir
Tastes
Humility within love.

Peppermint is humble with its healing art.
It has the Taste.

The wisdom within humility is infinite,
Spruce Tastes this.

Rosemary
Tastes the will of humility.
It is just what it is.

The Taste of humbleness within humility
Is what Elemi wood Tastes.

While the ability to Taste the manifestation of humility
Is within Pine.

Eucalyptus Tastes the harmony of humility.
&
Selenite Just Tastes
.

* NOW *
as
I TASTE

,

I RISE

.

Š Bell 20

The Nordic Child

As I Root,
I Now dance in the flow with all
.

I AM HUMILITY
&
* NOW *

I AM I AM
.
I AM I
.
I
JUST BE
.

Š Bell 21

The Hellenism Consort

Manifestation is a Baby Pink.
This is just the way I am loving it.

SAY
Yes, I Do
.

Just because I know I Love You.
This is all I do, even in times without a clue;
&
* NOW *
As I give my heart to everything
I FEEL
|
I am in union with my Majestic Wand.

The Divine Union,
With
I

.

.

.

Š *Bell* 22

The Hellenism Alchemist

I just be the performer in my enchantments;

I just be vulnerable when building my inner strength;

I just be the divine creation birthed with all my essences;

I just be the witness of my original innocence and love;

I just be devoted, while upholding my essence;

I just be the fountain of life who embraces all;

I just be in ceremony with my presence.

* NOW *
as
I FEEL

,

I RISE

.

Š Bell 23

The Hellenism Creator

Blood Orange
Feels ...
The Love in manifestation.

While my beloved Geranium
Feels the manifestation of innate healing.

The manifestation of wisdom,
Melissa Feels!

Manuka
Feels the manifestation of divine willpower,

while Balsam Peru
Feels the manifestation of humility.

Who Feels the manifestation within manifestation?
It is
Petitgrain.

Hinoki wood Feels...
The harmony manifested
&
Pink Mangano Just Feels.

* NOW *
as
I UNITE

...

I LIVE

.

Š *Bell* 24

The Hellenism Child

As I Co-create,
I Now unveil the love within all creations

·

I AM MANIFESTATION
&
* NOW *

I AM I AM

·

I AM I

·

I
JUST BE

·

Š Bell 25

The Cosmic Consort

Sacred Harmony is a Baby Rainbow.
This is just the way I am loving it.

SAY
Yes, I Do

.

Just because I know I Love You.
This is all I do, even in times without a clue;
&
* NOW *
As I give my heart to everything
I TOUCH

|

I am in union with my Sacred Story.

The Divine Union,
With
I

.

.

.

Š Bell 26

The Cosmic Alchemist

Dance and perform my touch of nothingness;

Dance until my vulnerableness dissolves;

Dance and birth love aloud, here and now;

Dance my harmonic melody within and without;

Dance my devotion until all my loves return Home as one;

Dance my union with my love flowing across the universe;

Dance Inter-dependently as one with all.

* NOW *
as
I TOUCH

,

I RISE

.

Š Bell 27

The Cosmic Creator

Palmarosa
Touches love with harmony,
and
harmony is what Vetiver heals through Touch.

Sacred Vanilla Touches ... wisdom of harmony,

While Amber Touches
the divine power within harmony.

Sandalwood is the one who Touches ...
humbleness within harmony.

Harmonic manifestation, the lotus Touches.

Om Ma! Tuberose,
Bless us through the infinite Touches
of
eternal harmony.
&
Herkimer Diamond Just Touches.

* NOW *
as
I JUST BE

...

I LIVE

.

Š Bell 28

The Cosmic Child

As I Rest,
I Now descend with my rainbow world
.

I AM SACRED HARMONY
&
NOW

I AM I AM
.

I AM I
.

I
JUST BE
.

.

.

HERE
:

One becomes two;

Two becomes three;

Three becomes seven;

Seven becomes all;

All become one

"I"
.

THE Š MATRIX

The Š Matrix is a metaphysical healing system. It is created to assist you to build a systematic foundation to live The Š philosophy, through targeting the healing at four levels within your being. By utilizing this healing system, you begin to release blockages within your light body and harmonize your being at all levels in a non-linear way. Hence, you re-embody your divinity while living in a world of duality in alignment.

This healing system is constructed with four metaphysical forms of healing:

1. **Spiritual Healing**—Š Love Notes.
2. **Physical Healing**—Š Plant Medicines.
3. **Mindful Healing**—Š Affirmations.
4. **Energetical Healing**—Š Rituals.

These metaphysical forms of healing aim for four results in us:

+ Heal the Inner Child.
+ Unify the Divine Masculine and Divine Feminine.
+ Reconnect with the Cosmic Child.
+ Re-embody as the Divine Child.

THE Š UNIVERSAL ARCHETYPES

	Venetian Facet	Celtic Facet	Indian Facet	Egyptian Facet	Nordic Facet	Hellenism Facet	Cosmic Facet
Lady Mary	Lady Mary	Aine	Rati	Isis	Freya	Aphrodite	Quan Yin
Mary Magdalene	Mary Magdalene	Airmed	Parvati	Bastet	Eir	Hestia	St. Germain
Green Tara	Green Tara	Danu	Saraswati	Hathor	Snotra	Athena	Lao Tzu
Black Madonna	Black Madonna	Ceridwen	Kali	Nephthys	Hel	Hecate	Metatron
Lady Fatima	Lady Fatima	Olwen	Aditi	Nut	Idun	Demeter	Melchizedek
Lady Nada	Lady Nada	Rhiannon	Lakshmi	Renenet	Gefjun	Gaia	Sanat Kumara
White Tara	White Tara	Brigid	Shakti	Maat	Sjofn	Iris	Maha Chohan

SPIRITUAL HEALING—Š LOVE NOTES

The Š Love Notes comprise wisdom translated directly from ciphers of the Š Dots. It is a spiritual method of healing. Every note is embedded with the wisdom of its corresponding universal archetype, each of which represents one of your forty-nine soul essences. These Š Love Notes are translated and written in modern human language, so you can understand the basic meaning of the ciphers −49 Š Dots. The Š Love Notes lead you to a deeper understanding of the 49 Š Dots and your soul essences. Ultimately, this form of metaphysical healing supports you in exploring your Divine Union.

Š Love Note 1

The Eternal Love Essence

♥

My Beloved,
Here I AM holding
"The Eternal Love Essence".
As you now see clearly, you can remember yours as well.

Finally!
Here you are deep within,
Where Love resides at your core.
Where Love is beyond an enchanted dream,
Where it is filled with infinite love with no end.

Remember,
The Truth includes all;
The beauty of living in duality is non-duality.
Through you understanding duality in your reality,
The miracle bestows, your heart now glows.

You are a virgin at your sacred heart

...

Dot to Dot;
Through mine to yours.
Strand by strand, you shall be
The eternal love that you truly are.

NOW,
Remember Your
"Once Upon A Dream"
&
Return As The Divine Child.

† *Lady Mary* †

Š Love Note 2

The Eternal Passion Essence

My Beloved,
Here I AM holding
"The Eternal Passion Essence".
As you now see clearly, you can remember yours as well.

Your true passion lies deep within your life force,
Come, cloak yourself in my rosette-adorned ruby-gown,
Feel my hot elixir dripping down to you,
Until your flame reignites and explodes.
We are all watching over you
As
You
Perform
The Now,
You open to Love ... Dance and Dance.

Unleash your heart desires.
Live your passion.
Be creative.

Can you feel my heart?
Can you feel my ecstasy?
Can you feel my creativity?
All In One Note.

NOW,
Be Merry & Make Merry.

† *Mary Magdalene* †

Š Love Note 3

The Eternal Divinity Essence

My Beloved,
Here I AM holding
"The Eternal Divinity Essence".
As you now see clearly, you can remember yours as well.

Gracefully, you strip down to your core-essence;
Naked you root at the pitch-black void;
Brightly, you shine on a Lotus-Rose.
In this state of Grace,
The Black Void,
Transforms,
Into

-

The Majestic Rainbow World,
Where all is loved.

You,
Who bare your whole being,
Bear divine miracles.
&
NOW,
Your
Light
Explodes
...
As The Love

-

Our Original State of Grace.

† *Green Tara* †

Š Love Note 4

The Eternal Pearl Essence

♥

My Beloved,
Here I AM holding
"The Eternal Pearl Essence".
As you now see clearly, you can remember yours as well.

Dot by Dot, Step by Step.
Pearl by Pearl, Thread by Thread.
You
Follow the whispers;
Follow the light;
Into The Void

.

At your core,
The Pearl,
You shall find.

NOW,
Descend with your rainbow light.
Walk in your essence of

...

The Eternal Pearl

.

Infinite divine beauties,
You Bestow
Now.

† *Black Madonna* †

Š Love Note 5

The Eternal Memoir Essence

♥

My Beloved,
Here I AM holding
"The Eternal Memoir Essence".
As you now see clearly, you can remember yours as well.

My Child,

Within
The One and Only
Book of Love
you came with,

Your Innocence unlocks
Your Sacred Story.

NOW,
Remember it, Rise with it.
Create it, Live it.

Be
IT

.

IT
Is

...

The
One & Only
LOVE.

† *Lady Fatima* †

Š *Love Note* 6

The Eternal Remembrance Essence

♥

My Beloved,
Here I AM holding
"The Eternal Remembrance Essence".
As you now see clearly, you can remember yours as well.

My Love,
May You Remember ...
Every turn of your birth,
Is The Divine Remembrance.

Every being
Is The Divine Expression
of
Love.

|

The Eternal Love.

NOW,
As you walk the infinite wheel,
You walk in the name of
LOVE

|

Where your Love is
Sealed
by
The Love.

† *Lady Nada* †

Š Love Note 7

The Eternal Conception Essence

♥

My Beloved,
Here I AM holding
"The Eternal Conception Essence".
As you now see clearly, you can remember yours as well.

My Love, The Divine Child
Is
YOU

,

Where I AM within
YOU

.

Shine your Rainbow Light.
Live your full sovereignty right
as a Divine Creation.

|

A facet of the Divine.

NOW,
As you paint your life with this rainbow,
The magnificent within you shall unveil itself

-

Come my Love ...
Drink my essence of
The Eternal Conception

...

Through birth and rebirth,
Three Become One.
You Are Whole
Now.

† *White Tara* †

Š *Love Note* 8

The Sacred Crib Essence

♥

My Beloved,
Here I AM holding
"The Sacred Crib Essence".
As you now see clearly, you can remember yours as well.

Lay down in Love.
Open your eyes,
I AM right in front of you.

Where glittering stars wrap around you,
Where The Star shines above you,
The Majestic Rainbow Love
Resides.

NOW,
You walk as a Star,
Loved From within
:
One become Two.
Two become Three.
Three become Four.
Four become All.
All Become
ONE
as
The Divine Child
...

† *Aine* †

Š Love Note 9

The Sacred Balm Essence

My Beloved,
Here I AM holding
"The Sacred Balm Essence".
As you now see clearly, you can remember yours as well.

Paint the Sacred Balm across the air,

The Majestic Rainbow

Unveils

Your divine umbrella.

NOW,
You

|

Under the divine umbrella,
As the Light Pillar,
You unify
Above & Below,
Within – Without.

.

.

.

All
As
ONE
I

.

† *Airmed* †

Š Love Note 10

The Sacred Chalice Essence

♥

My Beloved,
Here I AM holding
"The Sacred Chalice Essence".
As you now see clearly, you can remember yours as well.

Your Sacred Chalice

|

A Ruby-Red Essence

.

As it gently pulses,
From out of the Black Void
Your gnosis unveiled

.

This Gnosis Wisdom
Is
a selfless service to all.

NOW

...

Your
pearls of wisdoms fly across the universe,
land in those who open their heart.
To
Receive,
Listen,
Feel,
See
Love

|

My Love—Your Love—The Love.

† *Danu* †

Š *Love Note* 11

The Sacred Well Essence

My Beloved,
Here I AM holding
"The Sacred Well Essence".
As you now see clearly, you can remember yours as well.

The Sacred Well calls,
You answer.

Through The Dark, you see The Light;
Through The Light, you become The Love;
Through bathing in the Well, you birth and rebirth;
Through being The Love, you live your Divine Life.

Love includes both black and white;
Life includes both dark and light

...

Where black is white;
Dark is dissolved by the light.

&

NOW,
All Is Loved.

† *Ceridwen* †

Š Love Note 12

The Sacred Cloak Essence

My Beloved,
Here I AM holding
"The Sacred Cloak Essence".
As you now see clearly, you can remember yours as well.

As you strip down naked,
This cloak provides you with warmth.

Whenever you feel challenged,
This cloak gives you strength

.

Whenever you feel vulnerable,
This cloak cocoons you

.

Whenever you feel alone,
This Sacred Cloak becomes your beloved

.

Whenever You Come Home

...

This Sacred Cloak
Becomes
The Wedding Gown
You walk down the aisle with,
Surrendering as
The Bride of Love
Here & Now.

† *Olwen* †

Š *Love Note* 13

The Sacred Fountain Essence

My Beloved,
Here I AM holding
"The Sacred Fountain Essence".
As you now see clearly, you can remember yours as well.

Dipping into the Sacred Fountain,
You dissolve into nothingness.
Just Breathing,
Embracing

.

.

.

Here,
You Are Free.
You are Everything and Nothing

.

You
Who hold Infinite Divine Alchemy
Are
A fountain of Love
In
Life
Now

.

† *Rhiannon* †

Š Love Note 14

The Sacred Key Essence

♥

My Beloved,
Here I AM holding
"The Sacred Key Essence".
As you now see clearly, you can remember yours as well.

The Key to birthing infinite Divine Love
Is
within
The
Matrix of Duality.

Remember,
Laughers and Tears,
Joy and Sorrows,
Are all part of Love.

As we expand our hearts,
We become the love in duality.
As I drip my essence onto you,
The Sacred Key
You
Unlock
!
NOW,
Unleash your light at
The Infinite End.

† *Brigid* †

Š Love Note 15

The Magnificent Egg Essence

♥

My Beloved,
Here I AM holding
"The Magnificent Egg Essence".
As you now see clearly, you can remember yours as well.

The Magnificent Egg,
Resides within your sacred heart.

You
Rub, Rub, Rub

...

Up & Down,
Left & Right.
Your balance
Slowly swirl into place

...

Upon
The Crack of
Your Magnificent Egg.
|
You
Witness
The Miracles.
Love is born in you
NOW.

† *Rati* †

Š *Love Note* 16

The Magnificent Prism Essence

♥

My Beloved,
Here I AM holding
"The Magnificent Prism Essence".
As you now see clearly, you can remember yours as well.

At The Prism,
You Peep into Life.
The Majestic Rainbow Life,
A life filled with a spectrum of color.
You dance through the Divine gateways,
in a wink.

You
Unlock & Open
The gateway of life.
Filled with Unknowns;
Filled with Sacred Presents;
Filled with infinite Divine Miracles.

In a wink,
You return as The Magnificent Prism,
Your rainbow light now shines and glows.
You are a source of light,
You~NOW~Know.

† *Parvati* †

Š Love Note 17

The Magnificent Crown Essence

My Beloved,
Here I AM holding
"The Magnificent Crown Essence".
As you now see clearly, you can remember yours as well.

The Magnificent Crown
is
...
Above you
&
Below you
.

The key to holding the crown in duality
is
Balance.

Once in balance,
Union takes place;
Eternal Love Begins.

NOW,
You rebirth through The Void
with your rainbow sparkles
As
The
Divine
Child
HERE

.

† *Saraswati* †

Š *Love Note* 18

The Magnificent Chamber Essence

♥

My Beloved,
Here I AM holding
"The Magnificent Chamber Essence".
As you now see clearly, you can remember yours as well.

HERE,
You've Arrived at your chamber.
Your light reflects
like a mirror

...

Oh
Yes
!
You
Now
Remember

|

Who you truly are

;

Like a diamond
Shines through all illusions

.

NOW,
In The Magnificent Chamber,
Your rise with your horn blasting

:

With Love,
In Loved,
As Love.

† *Kali* †

Š Love Note 19

The Magnificent Bell Essence

♥

My Beloved,
Here I AM holding
"The Magnificent Bell Essence".
As you now see clearly, you can remember yours as well.

Strike the Magnificent Bell with love.
As it tinkles,
Love pours from all directions toward you.
You are loved just the way you are.

NOW,
In stillness

...

Feel the Love from all creations,
Honor each one of them,
Soak up all their love,
You become
The
Magnificent
Bell.

"Aloha"

.

You
Are
Alive
!

† *Aditi* †

Š *Love Note* 20

The Magnificent Lamp Essence

♥

My Beloved,
Here I AM holding
"The Magnificent Lamp Essence".
As you now see clearly, you can remember yours as well.

Under the umbrella of love,
I AM lighting up
The Magnificent Lamp.

See who you can See,
See what you can See,
See where you can See.
Simply,
Be happy with
All That You See.
!
Light up your Lamp
Hold it through all your
Twists & Turns

...

NOW,
Your
Magnificent
Shines As A Light To All.

† *Lakshmi* †

Š Love Note 21

The Magnificent Feather Essence

♥

My Beloved,
Here I AM holding
"The Magnificent Feather Essence".
As you now see clearly, you can remember yours as well.

As you dance with your feather
All creations unveil their light

...

One feather becomes Two.
Two Becomes Three.
Three Becomes Seven.
Seven Becomes Infinite

|

Where all
Comes
Back
To
One
!
NOW,
All creations awaken

|

Dance
Together
As
One Unified Love.

† *Shakti* †

Š Love Note 22

The Immortal Seal Essence

My Beloved,
Here I AM holding
"The Immortal Seal Essence".
As you now see clearly, you can remember yours as well.

The Immortal Seal
Is the seal of Divine Love.
Inscribed in your soul language.

As you stamp your seal

'

All

of

Creations

are

United

|

HERE

AS

ONE

"I"

...

Love is born

NOW

.

† *Isis* †

Š Love Note 23

The Immortal Womb Essence

My Beloved,
Here I AM holding
"The Immortal Womb Essence".
As you now see clearly, you can remember yours as well.

Spray around your potions;
Smell the beauty of all creations;
Dance in the flow of life, like the ocean.
Here,
I Anoint you with my essence

|

The grace
of
The Divine.
Sprinkle the majestic rainbow glitter as my omen.
NOW,
The Immortal Womb,
You Enter
As
The
Mother

.

† *Bastet* †

Š Love Note 24

The Immortal Thread Essence

My Beloved,
Here I AM holding
"The Immortal Thread Essence".
As you now see clearly, you can remember yours as well.

The Immortal Thread
resides within your love and your light.

Weave your Wisdom;   Weave our Union;   Weave your Power.
                Weave your Life;
                        Weave your Light;
                                        Weave your Sacred Story.
                Weave All Together.

Now,
Your rainbow light blasts.
                        All that I AM is woven
                As
                One
                Thread
                |
                I AM,
Your Immortal Thread.

† *Hathor* †

Š *Love Note* 25

The Immortal Charm Essence

My Beloved,
Here I AM holding
"The Immortal Charm Essence".
As you now see clearly, you can remember yours as well.

The Immortal Charm,
Your Remembrance

.

It holds the brightest light,
Shines through the darkest night.
Feel its grace,
Feel its love,
Just Feel

.

Now,
Upon your rebirth,
You Rise from The Void,
&
Light up the way.

† *Nephthys* †

Š Love Note 26

The Immortal Wings Essence

My Beloved,
Here I AM holding
"The Immortal Wings Essence".
As you now see clearly, you can remember yours as well.

You are a facet of the Divine,
beyond all roles you play in
"The Play".

As my wings touch yours,
You Birth; You Rise.
You bend to Fly.

Experience:
Above and Below;
Love, Light, and Life;
The Infinite and The Limitless
All in harmony under your wings.
Your wings touch lives
To Give Life.

Ready, Get set, Go.
Touch Lives,
Give Lives,
Live Life
Now
!

† *Nut* †

Š Love Note 27

The Immortal Halo Essence

My Beloved,
Here I AM holding
"The Immortal Halo Essence".
As you now see clearly, you can remember yours as well.

You Rise,
Your Halo Dance,
Your light bounces Up and Down.
Bounce and Bounce.
Listen to the rhythm within your heart,
All our soul symphonies are in harmony.
What a beauty
!
So
Listen
Deeply

,

Never Look Up
For Your Halo
!
The Immortal Halo

...

It's behind you;
It's all around you;
It's inside and outside of you.
You
Now
Uphold
!

† *Renenet* †

Š Love Note 28

The Immortal Scepter Essence

My Beloved,
Here I AM holding
"The Immortal Scepter Essence".
As you now see clearly, you can remember yours as well.

Upon
You anchored your Scepter,
The White dissolves The Black,
Your sacred feather arises.

NOW
The Majestic Rainbow is unveiled,
Door Opens; Path Clears.
Only Love You Hold
Now

...

Just
Play
On
Earth
HERE

,

Where life is the Lotus Rose.

† *Maat* †

Š *Love Note* 29

The Benevolent Star Essence

♥

My Beloved,
Here I AM holding
"The Benevolent Star Essence".
As you now see clearly, you can remember yours as well.

Twinkle, twinkle, little star

...

You

,

The Benevolent Star

|

A Seven-Pointed Star;
which
Shines through all illusions of
The Black and The White;
and
Glows in the Dark

.

NOW
I AM down to earth.
Your Star
Transforms
Into
A circle of rainbow delights.

|

The Rainbow World
You Embark On.

† *Freya* †

Š Love Note 30

The Benevolent Realm Essence

♥

My Beloved,
Here I AM holding
"The Benevolent Realm Essence".
As you now see clearly, you can remember yours as well.

The Benevolent Realm
Is wherever I AM.
It is within you,
IT
IS
YOU
!

When you reactivate this essence,
Whenever You Create,
Whatever You Touch,
Whoever You Are,
Wherever You Go
Is
SACRED
!

Now, you are
A facet of the Divine.

Here and Now,
You
Know
The Way
!

† *Eir* †

Š *Love Note* 31

The Benevolent Ark Essence

♥

My Beloved,
Here I AM holding
"The Benevolent Ark Essence".
As you now see clearly, you can remember yours as well.

All creations are interdependently one.
Like The Benevolent Ark.

|

We,

Beings,

As creations,

Are Divine Love

Uniquely Expressed.

We are part of the web of life,

Deeply interconnected at our core;

Playing different roles in The Divine Play.

A role is just a role.   Who we truly are is beyond all roles.

As we play these roles consciously, like a child,

we live beyond any limitation to

Experiencing

Divine

Love

In

Life

.

NOW
You flow like
The Benevolent Ark
Where You Are The Captain
Of Your Life.

† *Snotra* †

Š Love Note 32

The Benevolent Float Essence

♥

My Beloved,
Here I AM holding
"The Benevolent Float Essence".
As you now see clearly, you can remember yours as well.

From the pitch-black Void
You rise in waves.
As you soften your entire being,
Relax through all phases,
You float above all
Effortlessly.

NOW
Ride your life in waves

|

From One to Seven

;

From Seven to One

.

From One to Nothing

;

From
Nothing
to
Love
!

YOU ARE THE LOVE.

† *Hel* †

Š Love Note 33

The Benevolent Balloon Essence

♥

My Beloved,
Here I AM holding
"The Benevolent Balloon Essence".
As you now see clearly, you can remember yours as well.

Balloons are
Dancing and Flying,
In all directions

.

You
Jump
Up and Down

.

You catch every single balloon
To be rooted
Here & Now

.

NOW
You
Are
Love

.

Love
Is
You

.

YOU ARE FREE.

† *Idun* †

Š *Love Note* 34

The Benevolent Arrow Essence

♥

My Beloved,
Here I AM holding
"The Benevolent Arrow Essence".
As you now see clearly, you can remember yours as well.

Within the duality,
This Benevolent Arrow is what assists you
to be
Focused, Grounded, Connected.
Enabling you to live beyond illusions
while juggling life

.

NOW
Be
The Benevolent Arrow,
The Unmovable Love,
Stand through all thunder and lightning

...

Witness the Divine
Unfolding
Its
LOVE

.

Through its own
Time
&
Space
HERE.

† *Gefjun* †

Š *Love Note* 35

The Benevolent Carousel Essence

♥

My Beloved,
Here I AM holding
"The Benevolent Carousel Essence".
As you now see clearly, you can remember yours as well.

All creations are part of The Benevolent Carousel.
Fill it with Dots,
Fill it with Love,
Fill it with Colors

...

As you walk
Around and Around.
Your footprints are left as your dots;
Creating The New World
From dot to dot.

|

A world filled with
Dots,
Colors,
&
Love

.

NOW
All
Are
Living,
Loving,
Laughing,
In Perfect Harmony.

† *Sjofn* †

Š *Love Note* 36

The Divine Alchemy Essence

♥

My Beloved,
Here I AM holding
"The Divine Alchemy Essence".
As you now see clearly, you can remember yours as well.

You
Are
The Divine Alchemist

.

The Power is within you;
The Magic is within you;
The Love is within you

.

As
You
Stir & Stir
The Enchanted Cauldron

...

Bi ... Boo
!
Divine Creations
Are
Birthed
Through
You
|
One
As
I

.

† *Aphrodite* †

Š Love Note 37

The Divine Elixir Essence

♥

My Beloved,
Here I AM holding
"The Divine Elixir Essence".
As you now see clearly, you can remember yours as well.

Down the elixir,
Your being softens.

Now you are
The Divine Elixir.

You transform into water,
To touch the deepest
LOVE.

You transform into air,
To touch the utmost
LOVE
!

Now you touch,
All directions with
Your Essence
As
The
LOVE

.

† *Hestia* †

Š Love Note 38

The Divine Flame Essence

My Beloved,
Here I AM holding
"The Divine Flame Essence".
As you now see clearly, you can remember yours as well.

Sing, Sing, Sing,
Sing your soul song out loud.
Blast your love,
So
All
Can
Hear
!

Our horns are up,
Our lights are glowing,
Our passions are awakened
!
All our flames are ignited
At Once; At One

.

Once again we are
HERE and NOW
As One
|
At One
The Divine Flame
Ignites
!

† *Athena* †

Š Love Note 39

The Divine Labyrinth Essence

♥

My Beloved,
Here I AM holding
"The Divine Labyrinth Essence".
As you now see clearly, you can remember yours as well.

Light up Your Essence,
Light up Your Candle,
Light up Your Flame
|
Your Dandelion is unveiled,
Here,
Sprinkling glitter wherever you go.
NOW
Within The Divine Labyrinth,
You walk as Love in life
|
Walk
Until
"The Infinite End"

.

HERE
|
All Your Dreams
Are
Now
LIVED.

† *Hecate* †

Š *Love Note* 40

The Divine Gateway Essence

♥

My Beloved,
Here I AM holding
"The Divine Gateway Essence".
As you now see clearly, you can remember yours as well.

Here,
All our rainbow threads
weave together as The Sacred Heart

.

The Divine Gateway opens.
We Are Free

!

We
Live
The
Eternal
Love

...

NOW
All our rainbow lights
SHINE
As
ONE
LIGHT

.

† *Demeter* †

Š *Love Note* 41

The Divine Flower Essence

My Beloved,
Here I AM holding
"The Divine Flower Essence".
As you now see clearly, you can remember yours as well.

Dance
in
Your
Heart
as
The Divine Flower
|
The soulful medicine
Vibrates

.

This Bloom
Makes
Your heart bloom

...

NOW
|
The Eternal Love
Begins

.

HERE
At the Infinite End,
You
Flourish like
The Rainbow Diamond.

† *Gaia* †

Š *Love Note* 42

The Divine Drum Essence

♥

My Beloved,
Here I AM holding
"The Divine Drum Essence".
As you now see clearly, you can remember yours as well.

Drum Your Divine Drum,

Surrender & Flow.

Flow Through The White,

To feel your purity.

Flow Through The Black,

To explore your magnificent.

Flow, Flow, Flow.
Experience The Divine

|

You Are Love.

HERE,
As
The Child.
Drum beyond The Black and The White,
Blast all with your rainbow delights.
NOW
You
Say
"Thank You"
To All
!

† *Iris* †

Š Love Note 43

The Majestic Orchestration Essence

♥ ♥ ♥　♥ ♥

My Beloved,
Here I AM holding
"The Majestic Orchestration Essence".
As you now see clearly, you can remember yours as well.

The Majestic Orchestration
|
Strings of your soul:
The seven rainbow strings.
When playing this harmonic vibration,
The Divine, you shall feel

...

As
YOU
PLAY
HERE

,

All creations unfold;
Like the rainbow you behold.

NOW
Miracles Bestow

...

Just because you
Fall in love
Long,
Long
Ago
!

† *Quan Yin* †

Š Love Note 44

The Majestic Freedom Essence

♥ ♥ ♥ ♥ ♥

My Beloved,
Here I AM holding
"The Majestic Freedom Essence".
As you now see clearly, you can remember yours as well.

Through The White,
You see The Black.
Through The Black,
You see The White.
Through The Black & White,
You see beyond all veils
&
Show up
As
The
Love
.

Here & Now
You Are Free
!

Free to experience your magnificence
As Divine Love.
Free to experience your divinity
Just the way it is.
Free to experience divine miracles.
Where All Is Love
|
The Divine Life,
You Live.

† *St. Germain* †

Š Love Note 45

The Majestic Wisdom Essence

♥ ♥ ♥ ♥ ♥

My Beloved,
Here I AM holding
"The Majestic Wisdom Essence".
As you now see clearly, you can remember yours as well.

Your Non-linear way of living,
Unlocks your divinity

...

NOW
Together,
You Reclaim
Your sovereignty,
Your compass in life

...

HERE
You Transform
The Presence into your presents

.

The Majestic Wisdom,
Includes the Truth of All

.

Your Truth,
My Truth,
All Truths.

† *Lao Tzu* †

Š Love Note 46

The Majestic Immortality Essence

♥ ♥ ♥   ♥ ♥

My Beloved,
Here I AM holding
"The Majestic Immortality Essence".
As you now see clearly, you can remember yours as well.

Your Eternal Dream
Holds The Immortal Light

...

HERE
You
Swirl
Into
Harmony

.

Love Births Through Duality

.

NOW
The Majestic Immortality brings to you

:

The Divine Order, The Infinite Light, The Eternal Dream

|

Where all sacraments are lived

...

Your World,
My World,
As
ONE
WORLD

!

† *Metatron* †

Š Love Note 47

The Majestic Order Essence

My Beloved,
Here I AM holding
"The Majestic Order Essence".
As you now see clearly, you can remember yours as well.

The Majestic Order
Resides in the sacred heart.
Where shapes and forms are Inscribed as the language.
Through Your Feelings;
Through The Whispers;
Through The Presence;
You Feel;

You Listen;

You Understand;

You Are The Present
!
HERE
You explore The Majestic Order.
You experience the divine world.
You experiment with magnificent creations
You expedite
The Eternal Dream
!
NOW
Simply
say
"Yes, I Do."

† *Melchizedek* †

Š *Love Note* 48

The Majestic Union Essence

♥ ♥ ♥   ♥ ♥

My Beloved,
Here I AM holding
"The Majestic Union Essence".
As you now see clearly, you can remember yours as well.

Divine Union is where

White is within Black,

Black is within White.

The Majestic Rainbow
Is The Core.

NOW

...

ONE,
TWO,
THREE,
FOUR,
FIVE,
SIX,
SEVEN.

HERE
At Seven,
We Are Reborn As
One
I

.

Happy Birthday !

† *Sanat Kumara* †

Š Love Note 49

The Majestic World Essence

♥ ♥ ♥ ♥ ♥

My Beloved,
Here I AM holding
"The Majestic World Essence".
As you now see clearly, you can remember yours as well.

The Pathways to live as Love are
Infinite;
It is your birthright to live it
!
The Colors of your Rainbow Diamond are
Infinite;
It is your birthright to rise with all
!
The Key to create Divine Creations is
Seven;
It is your birth right to create majesty
!
The Wisdom you came with holds
Miracles;
It is your birthright to just be you
!
HERE
The dream behind the Earth is within
Your
Majestic World
!
NOW
At The Infinite End,
I AM The Divine Child.

† *Maha Chohan* †

THE Š PLANT MEDICINES

Venetian Facet	Jasmine	Ylang Ylang	Davana	Benzoin	Lavender	Niaouli	Neroli
Celtic Facet	Rose	Juniper Berry	Clary Sage	Raven Sara	Bergamot	Cedarwood	Patchouli
Indian Facet	Coriander	Cinnamon	Cardamom	Nutmeg	Clove	Pepper	Ginger
Egyptian Facet	Frankincense	Myrrh	Cistus	Hyssop	Copaiba	Galbanum	Cypress
Nordic Facet	Fir	Peppermint	Spruce	Rosemary	Elemi Wood	Pine	Eucalyptus
Hellenism Facet	Blood Orange	Geranium	Melissa	Manuka	Balsam Peru	Petitgrain	Hinoki Wood
Cosmic Facet	Palmarosa	Vetiver	Vanilla	Amber	Sandalwood	Lotus	Tuberose

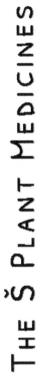

PHYSICAL HEALING—Š PLANT MEDICINE

"Š Plant Medicines" is a physical method of healing. Each medicinal plant is chosen specifically to support you as you walk each of the corresponding "49 Š steps". Through walking these Š steps, you will retrieve your sacred gifts from the divine. Each plant medicine holds a unique ability to assist your physical body to reconnect and anchor with Divine Love. All these plant medicines are teachers to assist you in deepening your understanding of your diamond light body, especially on your physical level. Ultimately, this form of metaphysical healing supports you in reconnecting with your divinity at all levels.

Š Plant Medicine 1
Jasmine ♥

Color Ray: Purple

Divine Facet: The Venetian Facet

Sacred Gifts: Purity

*Hint: Divine magnetism is invoked from the centre of your being.

Š Plant Medicine 2
Ylang Ylang ♥

Color Ray: Purple

Divine Facet: The Venetian Facet

Sacred Gifts: Passion

*Hint: Passion flows through the dance of your soul.

Š Plant Medicine 3
Davana ♥

Color Ray: Purple

Divine Facet: The Venetian Facet

Sacred Gifts: The Sacred Flame

*Hint: Bask in the warmth of the Sacred Eternal Flame.

Š Plant Medicine 4
Benzoin ♥

Color Ray: Purple

Divine Facet: The Venetian Facet

Sacred Gifts: Blessing

*Hint: Blessed Be, Namaste, Amen.

Š PLANT MEDICINE 5
Lavender ♥

Color Ray: Purple

Divine Facet: The Venetian Facet

Sacred Gifts: Soul Symphony

*Hint: Sing your Soul Song in the harmonic breath of creation.

Š PLANT MEDICINE 6
Niaouli ♥

Color Ray: Purple

Divine Facet: The Venetian Facet

Sacred Gifts: Purification

*Hint: Bask in the sacred cleansing waves of Mother Nature.

Š PLANT MEDICINE 7
Neroli ♥

Color Ray: Purple

Divine Facet: The Venetian Facet

Sacred Gifts: Self-Mastery

*Hint: The sound of truth lives inside of you.

Š PLANT MEDICINE 8
Rose ♥

Color Ray: Blue

Divine Facet: The Celtics Facet

Sacred Gifts: Self-love

*Hint: Your self-loving actions open up infinite doorways.

Š Plant Medicine 9
Juniper Berry

Color Ray: Blue

Divine Facet: The Celtics Facet

Sacred Gifts: Boundaries

*Hint: What's your YES & NO?

Š Plant Medicine 10
Clary Sage

Color Ray: Blue

Divine Facet: The Celtics Facet

Sacred Gifts: Divination

*Hint: Share your awakened oracular gifts with the world.

Š Plant Medicine 11
Revensara

Color Ray: Blue

Divine Facet: The Celtics Facet

Sacred Gifts: Courage

*Hint: Trust and act upon your inner knowing.

Š Plant Medicine 12
Bergamot

Color Ray: Blue

Divine Facet: The Celtics Facet

Sacred Gifts: Grace

*Hint: All your six senses are activated to experience Grace.

Š PLANT MEDICINE 13
Cedarwood ♥

Color Ray: Blue

Divine Facet: The Celtics Facet

Sacred Gifts: Clarity

*Hint: Clear insights are revealed through your meditations.

Š PLANT MEDICINE 14
Patchouli ♥

Color Ray: Blue

Divine Facet: The Celtics Facet

Sacred Gifts: Alchemy

*Hint: Divine Creation is birthing through you now.

Š PLANT MEDICINE 15
Coriander ♥

Color Ray: Green

Divine Facet: The Indian Facet

Sacred Gifts: Clearance

*Hint: Clear your inner and outer world with loving presence.

Š PLANT MEDICINE 16
Cinnamon ♥

Color Ray: Green

Divine Facet: The Indian Facet

Sacred Gifts: Power

*Hint: Reclaim your divine sovereignty.

Š PLANT MEDICINE 17
Cardamom ♥

Color Ray: Green

Divine Facet: The Indian Facet

Sacred Gifts: Present

*Hint: All is revealed in the beauty of doing nothing.

Š PLANT MEDICINE 18
Nutmeg ♥

Color Ray: Green

Divine Facet: The Indian Facet

Sacred Gifts: Miracles

*Hint: Miracles are birthing through you.

Š PLANT MEDICINE 19
Clove Buds ♥

Color Ray: Green

Divine Facet: The Indian Facet

Sacred Gifts: Surrender

*Hint: You are mastering the flow of your life.

Š PLANT MEDICINE 20
Pepper ♥

Color Ray: Green

Divine Facet: The Indian Facet

Sacred Gifts: Contemplation

*Hint: Dream your dreams; your boundless dreams.

Š PLANT MEDICINE 21
Ginger ♥

Color Ray: Green

Divine Facet: The Indian Facet

Sacred Gifts: Enthusiasm

*Hint: Your inner soul fire is fuelling up for your creative actions.

Š PLANT MEDICINE 22
Frankincense

Color Ray: Yellow

Divine Facet: The Egyptian Facet

Sacred Gifts: The Innocence

*Hint: Your original epigenetic DNA are being reactivated.

Š PLANT MEDICINE 23
Myrrh

Color Ray: Yellow

Divine Facet: The Egyptian Facet

Sacred Gifts: The Healer

*Hint: Your inner healing ability has been further activated.

Š PLANT MEDICINE 24
Cistus

Color Ray: Yellow

Divine Facet: The Egyptian Facet

Sacred Gifts: Gratitude

*Hint: Your gratitude has opened a powerful doorway to love.

Š PLANT MEDICINE 25
Hyssop

Color Ray: Yellow

Divine Facet: The Egyptian Facet

Sacred Gifts: Rebirth

*Hint: Your divine self-birthing process is happening now.

Š PLANT MEDICINE 26
Copaiba

Color Ray: Yellow

Divine Facet: The Egyptian Facet

Sacred Gifts: Freedom

*Hint: The essence of your spirit is boundless.

Š PLANT MEDICINE 27
Galbanum

Color Ray: Yellow

Divine Facet: The Egyptian Facet

Sacred Gifts: New Life

*Hint: Your new way of living is about to emerge.

Š PLANT MEDICINE 28
Cypress

Color Ray: Yellow

Divine Facet: The Egyptian Facet

Sacred Gifts: Initiation

*Hint: A doorway to your soul's attunement is opening now.

Š PLANT MEDICINE 29
Fir ♥

Color Ray: Orange

Divine Facet: The Nordic Facet

Sacred Gifts: Revival

*Hint:** Be your own inner gardener and start planting.

Š PLANT MEDICINE 30
Peppermint ♥

Color Ray: Orange

Divine Facet: The Nordic Facet

Sacred Gifts: Peace

*Hint:** Peace comes on your wings of breath.

Š PLANT MEDICINE 31
Spruce ♥

Color Ray: Orange

Divine Facet: The Nordic Facet

Sacred Gifts: Ceremony

*Hint:** Perform a sacred ceremony just for yourself.

Š PLANT MEDICINE 32
Rosemary ♥

Color Ray: Orange

Divine Facet: The Nordic Facet

Sacred Gifts: The Soul Remembrance

*Hint:** Your soul story awaits ....

Š PLANT MEDICINE 33
Elemi Wood ♥

Color Ray: Orange

Divine Facet: The Nordic Facet

Sacred Gifts: Well-Being

*Hint: Nourishing your body is an act of self-love.

Š PLANT MEDICINE 34
Pine ♥

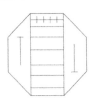

Color Ray: Orange

Divine Facet: The Nordics Facet

Sacred Gifts: Aspirations

*Hint: Awaken to your divine guidance and soul goals.

Š PLANT MEDICINE 35
Eucalyptus ♥

Color Ray: Orange

Divine Facet: The Nordic Facet

Sacred Gifts: Creativities

*Hint: Unleash the artist within and wield your imagination.

Š PLANT MEDICINE 36
Blood Orange ♥

Color Ray: Pink

Divine Facet: The Hellenism Facet

Sacred Gifts: Playfulness

*Hint: Life is a play; become your own leading light.

Š PLANT MEDICINE 37
Geranium ♥

Color Ray: Pink

Divine Facet: The Hellenism Facet

Sacred Gifts: Revelation

*Hint: Come out of the closet; reveal your true beauty.

Š PLANT MEDICINE 38
Melissa ♥

Color Ray: Pink

Divine Facet: The Hellenism Facet

Sacred Gifts: Enchantment

*Hint: You are unfurling new worlds into being with your pure expression.

Š PLANT MEDICINE 39
Manuka ♥

Color Ray: Pink

Divine Facet: The Hellenism Facet

Sacred Gifts: Sweetness

*Hint: Rainbow delight radiates through your being.

Š PLANT MEDICINE 40
Balsam Peru ♥

Color Ray: Pink

Divine Facet: The Hellenism Facet

Sacred Gifts: Prosperity

*Hint: You are receiving beautiful abundance on all levels.

Š PLANT MEDICINE 41
Petitgrain ♥

Color Ray: Pink

Divine Facet: The Hellenism Facet

Sacred Gifts: Joy

*Hint: Moment to moment, let joy live through you.

Š PLANT MEDICINE 42
Hinoki wood ♥

Color Ray: Pink

Divine Facet: The Hellenism Facet

Sacred Gifts: Stillness

*Hint: In stillness, you realized the beauty of life.

Š PLANT MEDICINE 43
Palmarosa ♥ ♥ ♥ ♥ ♥

Color Ray: Rainbow

Divine Facet: The Cosmic Facet

Sacred Gifts: Cooperation

*Hint: Hand-in-hand, we co-create pure love on earth.

Š PLANT MEDICINE 44
Vetiver ♥ ♥ ♥ ♥ ♥

Color Ray: Rainbow

Divine Facet: The Cosmic Facet

Sacred Gifts: Alignment

*Hint: Align with your inner divine as your ground.

Š PLANT MEDICINE 45
Vanilla ♥ ♥ ♥ ♥ ♥

Color Ray: Rainbow

Divine Facet: The Cosmic Facet

Sacred Gifts: Sacred Sanctuary

*Hint: I AM loved; I AM safe.

Š PLANT MEDICINE 46
Amber ♥ ♥ ♥ ♥ ♥

Color Ray: Rainbow

Divine Facet: The Cosmic Facet

Sacred Gifts: Wisdom

*Hint: Divine gnosis blossoms from the depth of your soul.

Š PLANT MEDICINE 47
Sandalwood ♥ ♥ ♥ ♥ ♥

Color Ray: Rainbow

Divine Facet: The Cosmic Facet

Sacred Gifts: Serenity

*Hint: You are the Queen of your own Queendom.

Š PLANT MEDICINE 48
Lotus ♥ ♥ ♥ ♥ ♥

Color Ray: Rainbow

Divine Facet: The Cosmic Facet

Sacred Gifts: Compassion

*Hint: With compassion, you accept all of life exactly as it is.

Š PLANT MEDICINE 49

Tuberose ♥ ♥ ♥ ♥ ♥

Color Ray: Rainbow

Divine Facet: The Cosmic Facet

Sacred Gifts: Celebration

*Hint: Your divine rainbow radiance is in absolute alignment.

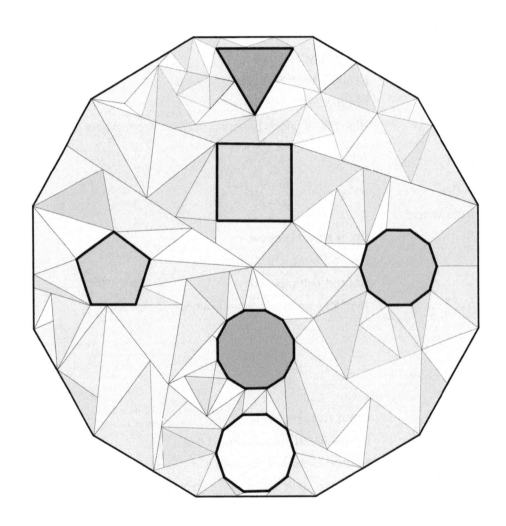

"Š Plant 0 – I AM I"

The Š Algorithm of Divine Presence

	I AM	Listener	Forgivness	Humility	Compassion	Sacret Heart	Acceptance
Perform							
Vulnerate	Performance	Authenticity	Empowerment	Ground	Courage	Passion	Contemplation
Birth	Performance	Vulnerableness	Realization	Breath	Play	Create	Surrender
Witness	Performance	Vulnerableness	Birth	Release	Dance	Pray	Flow
Devotion	Performance	Vulnerableness	Birth	Witness	Grace	Curiosity	Enchantment
Union	Performance	Vulnerableness	Birth	Witness	Devotion	Embrace	Ceremony
Just Be	Performance	Vulnerableness	Birth	Witness	Devotion	Union	Live

Mindful Healing—Š Affirmations

As a mindful method of healing, "The Š Affirmations" is designed to motivate you to live with your divine presence in every moment. These affirmations are written to support your alignment through rebalancing and rewiring your mind during the ups and downs in life. "The Š Affirmations" is categorized by the seven divine presences, which are:

PERFORM ♥
   Represented by Š Affirmation Nos. 1-7.

VULNERABLENESS ♥
   Represented by Š Affirmation Nos. 8-14.

BIRTH ♥
   Represented by Š Affirmation Nos. 15-21.

WITNESS
   Represented by Š Affirmation Nos. 22-28.

DEVOTION ♥
   Represented by Š Affirmation Nos. 29-35.

UNION ♥
   Represented by Š Affirmation Nos. 36-42.

JUST BE ♥ ♥ ♥　♥ ♥
   Represented by Š Affirmation Nos. 43-49.

Ultimately, this form of metaphysical healing supports you in rebirthing your being in wholeness.

Š AFFIRMATION 1 ♥
Alignment
> I AM Love, I AM light, I AM grace, I AM Love.

Š AFFIRMATION 2 ♥
Listen
> I AM listening deeply. I hear you, my beloved, I AM listening deeply.

Š AFFIRMATION 3 ♥
Forgiveness
> I AM forgiveness. I forgive myself, I forgive all, I AM forgiveness.

Š AFFIRMATION 4 ♥
Humility
> I AM humble. I walk with humility, I live life with humility, I AM humble.

Š AFFIRMATION 5 ♥
Compassion
> I AM compassion. I am worthy of compassion, I Live with compassion, I AM compassion.

Š AFFIRMATION 6 ♥
Sacred Heart
> I AM the sacred heart. I love with my heart, I live in the heart, I AM the sacred heart.

Š AFFIRMATION 7 ♥
Acceptance
> I AM who I AM. I accept all that I AM, I accept who I truly AM, I AM who I AM.

Š AFFIRMATION 8 ♥
Performance
> Even in time of my vulnerableness, I AM the divine performer.

Š AFFIRMATION 9 ♥
Authenticity
> Even in time of my vulnerableness, I AM authentic.

Š AFFIRMATION 10 ♥
Empowerment
> Even in time of my vulnerableness, I AM empowered.

Š AFFIRMATION 11 ♥
Ground
> Even in time of my vulnerableness, I AM grounded.

Š AFFIRMATION 12 ♥
Courage
> Even in time of my vulnerableness, I AM courageous.

Š AFFIRMATION 13 ♥
Passion
> Even in time of my vulnerableness, I am passionate.

Š AFFIRMATION 14 ♥
Dream
> Even in time of my vulnerableness, I AM a divine dreamer.

Š AFFIRMATION 15 ♥
Performance
> Through my performance, I AM all that I AM.

Š AFFIRMATION 16 ♥
Vulnerableness
> Through my vulnerableness, I open up to the divine conception.

Š AFFIRMATION 17 ♥
Realization
> Through my sacred heart, I realize love is born in me.

Š AFFIRMATION 18 ♥
Breath
> Through breathing, birthing becomes effortless.

Š AFFIRMATION 19 ♥
Play
> Through birthing divine creations, I just play.

Š AFFIRMATION 20 ♥
Create
> Through rebirthing, I create my divine life.

Š AFFIRMATION 21 ♥
Surrender
> Through surrendering, I AM born.

Š AFFIRMATION 22
Performance
> As I perform in love, I witness divine miracles.

Š AFFIRMATION 23
Vulnerableness
> As I embrace my vulnerableness, I build up strengths within me.

Š AFFIRMATION 24
Birth
> As I give birth, I witness my magnificence as a divine creation.

Š AFFIRMATION 25
Release
> As I become a witness of the divine, I let go of who I believe I AM.

Š AFFIRMATION 26
Dance
> As I witness divine miracles, I dance through life effortlessly.

Š AFFIRMATION 27
Prayer
> As I pray in the name of love, I witness Divine Love within and without.

Š AFFIRMATION 28
Flow
> As I flow in life with all creations, I AM the witness of who I AM.

Š AFFIRMATION 29 ♥
Performance
    I AM devoted to perform in the divine play.

Š AFFIRMATION 30 ♥
Vulnerableness
    I AM devoted to accept all vulnerableness in the name of Love.

Š AFFIRMATION 31 ♥
Birth
    I AM devoted to birth divine creations.

Š AFFIRMATION 32 ♥
Witness
    I AM devoted to witnessing all divine magnificence.

Š AFFIRMATION 33 ♥
Grace
    I AM devoted to being grace.

Š AFFIRMATION 34 ♥
Curiosity
    I AM devoted to staying curious at all times.

Š AFFIRMATION 35 ♥
Enchantment
    I AM devoted to being the enchantment of life.

Š AFFIRMATION 36 ♥
Performance
> I now perform for life in divine union. I AM I AM.

Š AFFIRMATION 37 ♥
Vulnerableness
> I now live my vulnerableness through my divine union. I AM I AM.

Š AFFIRMATION 38 ♥
Birth
> I now give birth through my divine union within. I AM I AM.

Š AFFIRMATION 39 ♥
Witness
> I now witness the divine union within and without. I AM I AM.

Š AFFIRMATION 40 ♥
Devotion
> I now devote my entire being as part of the divine union. I AM I AM.

Š AFFIRMATION 41 ♥
Embrace
> I now embrace all of life through the divine union. I AM I AM.

Š AFFIRMATION 42 ♥
Ceremony
> I now live life in divine union as a ceremony. I AM I AM.

Š AFFIRMATION 43 ♥ ♥ ♥ ♥ ♥
Performance
> I just be and perform all my roles in the divine play. I AM I.

Š AFFIRMATION 44 ♥ ♥ ♥ ♥ ♥
Vulnerableness
> I just be, even when I am feeling vulnerable. I AM I.

Š AFFIRMATION 45 ♥ ♥ ♥ ♥ ♥
Birth
> I just be the Divine Love birthed from the divine. I AM I.

Š AFFIRMATION 46 ♥ ♥ ♥ ♥ ♥
Witness
> I just be the witness of all divine miracles. I AM I.

Š AFFIRMATION 47 ♥ ♥ ♥ ♥ ♥
Devotion
> I just be, who I truly AM. I AM I.

Š AFFIRMATION 48 ♥ ♥ ♥ ♥ ♥
Union
> I just be the Divine Union within and without. I AM I.

Š AFFIRMATION 49 ♥ ♥ ♥ ♥ ♥
Live
> I just be present in life, living the life. I AM I.

THE Š RITUALS

	Energy Transmission	Mindful Affirmation	Selfcare Ritual	Body Activation	Dietary Boost	Creative Alchemy	Light Body Reset
Venetian Facet	The Eternal Flame Invocation	Perform	Hair Care	Standing Qigong	Lotus	A Dot	14:10 Fasting + Green Soup
Celtic Facet	The Eternal Flame Invocation	Vulnerate	Womb Spa	Gentle walk	Mushroom	A Dot	16:8 Fasting + Buckwheat soup
Indian Facet	The Eternal Flame Invocation	Birth	Oral Renewal	Stretching	Cannellini Beans	A Dot	20:4 Fasting + Lentil Soup
Egyptian Facet	The Eternal Flame Invocation	Witness	Aura Rebalance	Strength Training	Black Rice	A Dot	High Fibre Liquid Diet
Nordic Facet	The Eternal Flame Invocation	Devotion	Medicinal Bath	Floatation Therapy	Cherry	A Dot	High Omega Liquid Diet
Hellenism Facet	The Eternal Flame Invocation	Union	Facial Renewal	Sacred Dance	Fig	A Dot	High Protein Liquid Diet
Cosmic Facet	The Eternal Flame Invocation	Just Be	Body Adornment	Breathwork	Cacao	A Dot	24 Hour Fasting

Energetic Healing—Š Rituals

"The Š Rituals" is an energetic method of healing. This method consists of forty-nine spiritual practices you can execute daily to expand and re-balance your light body, to keep you in alignment. These practices are organized into seven categories:

+ Energy Transmission,
+ Mindful Affirmation,
+ Self-Care Ritual,
+ Body Activation,
+ Dietary Boost,
+ Creative Alchemy,
+ Light Body Reset.

Each Š Ritual is served as a portal, to alchemize your light from the form of energy vibration into a state of matter in life. Each practice is interconnected with the Š Matrix. Each holds a unique healing ability, and each provides you a way to live the Š philosophy daily.

ENERGY TRANSMISSION

This category of rituals brings you healing through energy transmission. To execute the rituals, read the invocation of The Eternal Flame aloud and sit in its healing energy. This approach activates the energy transmissions through the sound waves of your voice and the energy embedded within each chosen word. This flame holds the healing ability that harmonizes your light body, and makes space for Divine Love to be anchored within you.

MINDFUL AFFIRMATION

This category of rituals brings you healing through mindful affirmation. It requires you to read the Š Affirmations aloud in order to rebalance your mental body, refine your soul alignment, and provide you with the inner strength and willpower to move forward in life.

SELF-CARE RITUAL

This category of rituals brings you healing through self-care. It is a creative process you can customize according to your understanding of your body's intelligence. You can use natural ingredients available around you in different seasons to assist you in listening more deeply to your body and deepen your understanding of the Earth.

BODY ACTIVATION

This category of rituals brings you healing through body activation. It comprises different strength-of-body movements that assist you in anchoring Divine Love in your physical body. The rituals aim to release blockages and help you build up physical stamina, thereby enabling you to uphold your rainbow diamond light at all levels within duality on Earth.

DIETARY BOOST

This category of rituals brings you healing through dietary boost. It encourages you to go deep into understanding the divine intelligence of each sacred plant through your creativities. The rituals also assist you re-embody your divine wisdom as well as boosting your physical body correspondingly.

CREATIVE ALCHEMY

This category of rituals brings you healing through creative alchemy. It is derived from the Š Dots and the Š Love Notes. All creations are birthed from a dot of Divine Love, and we are all granted the freedom to create more love in life from the original dot.

LIGHT BODY RESET

This category of rituals brings you healing through a reset of your light body. It is formulated to support your whole light body to rest and reset through intermittent fasting, a micronutrient diet, and a liquid diet.

There is more than one way to utilize The Š Rituals. The simplest way is to follow the sacred practices from Day 1 to 49, as a 49-day healing retreat. You are encouraged to tap into your intuition and creativity to design your bespoke retreats by combining practices from the Š Rituals. Hence, this leads you to expedite your ascension and become the Divine Child.
***Hint:** You can design healing retreats for yourself based on these numbers: 7, 14, 21, 28, 35, 42, 49. Your intuition is the key here to create.*

WEEK 1 ♥

Day 1: Energy Transmission: The Eternal Flame Invocation.
Day 2: Mindful Affirmation: *Perform*—Affirmation Nos.1–7.
Day 3: Self-Care: Hair Care.
Day 4: Body Activation: Standing Qi-Gong.
Day 5: Dietary Boost: Lotus.
Day 6: Creative Alchemy: Create anything from a dot of love within you.
Day 7: Light Body Reset: 14:10 hours Intermittent fasting with green soup.

WEEK 2 ♥

Day 1: Energy Transmission: The Eternal Flame Invocation.
Day 2: Mindful Affirmation: *Vulnerableness*—Affirmation Nos. 8–14.
Day 3: Self-Care: Womb Spa.
Day 4: Body Activation: Gentle walk.
Day 5: Dietary Boost: Mushroom.
Day 6: Creative Alchemy: Create anything from a dot of love within you.
Day 7: Light Body Reset 16:8 hours Intermittent fasting with buckwheat soup.

WEEK 3 ♥

Day 1: Energy Transmission: The Eternal Flame Invocation.
Day 2: Mindful Affirmation: *Birth*—Affirmation Nos. 15–21.
Day 3: Self-Care: Oral Renewal.
Day 4: Body Activation: Stretching.
Day 5: Dietary Boost: Cannellini Beans.
Day 6: Creative Alchemy: Create anything from a dot of love within you.
Day 7: Light Body Reset 20:4 hours Intermittent fasting with lentil soup.

WEEK 4

Day 1: Energy Transmission: The Eternal Flame Invocation.
Day 2: Mindful Affirmation: *Witness*—Affirmation Nos. 22–28.
Day 3: Self-Care: Aura rebalancing.
Day 4: Body Activation: Strength training.
Day 5: Dietary Boost: Black rice.
Day 6: Creative Alchemy: Create anything from a dot of love within you.
Day 7: Light Body Reset: High-fiber liquid diet.

WEEK 5 ♥

Day 1: Energy Transmission: The Eternal Flame invocation.
Day 2: Mindful Affirmation: *Devotion—*Affirmation Nos. 29–35.
Day 3: Self-Care: Medicinal bath.
Day 4: Body Activation: Float therapy.
Day 5: Dietary Boost: Cherries.
Day 6: Creative Alchemy: Create anything from a dot of love within you.
Day 7: Light Body Reset: High-omega liquid diet.

WEEK 6 ♥

Day 1: Energy Transmission: The Eternal Flame Invocation.
Day 2: Mindful Affirmation: *Union—*Affirmation Nos. 36–42.
Day 3: Self-Care: Facial renewal.
Day 4: Body Activation: Sacred dance.
Day 5: Dietary Boost: Figs.
Day 6: Creative Alchemy: Create anything from a dot of love within you.
Day 7: Light Body Reset: High-protein liquid diet.

WEEK 7 ♥ ♥ ♥ ♥ ♥

Day 1: Energy Transmission: The Eternal Flame Invocation.
Day 2: Mindful Affirmation: *Just Be—*Affirmation Nos. 43–49.
Day 3: Self-Care: Body adornment.
Day 4: Body Activation: Breathwork.
Day 5: Dietary Boost: Cacao.
Day 6: Creative Alchemy: Create anything from a dot of love within you.
Day 7: Light Body Reset: 24 hours fasting.

THE Š TESTIMONY

My beloved children,

Now is the divine time to share with you my testimonies—The Š Testimony. These are written based on my personal experiences derived from my communion with the Divine. These twenty-eight testimonials are served as a portal for you to experience the Divine through my communion—bringing my Majestic Rainbow Orchestration alive in life.

Living your divinity isn't just about the self-realizations you attained—your process and your unique experiences are equally important. During this process of living The Š philosophy, you will encounter divine miracles; You will also experience the magnificence of the divine and yourself as a divine being. Moreover, all the sacred stories you live, all the love you embody, all the divine things you create, and all the self-realizations you attain, hold immense healing powers that can be shared with our humanity. Living The Š philosophy provides you ways to love our humanity as a selfless-service on Earth.

Grandma MA.

Š Testimony I

The Eternal Love

The moment you touch me,
I remember you, but I don't know you.
You feel outside of me,   but I know you are deep within me.
You know me inside out,   but I don't seem to know you.
Who are you? Who AM I?

I look deep into your soul, and realize it is my soul.
Have we met?
In moments of "I Don't Know,"
Honesty is what I have left to show.
But I honestly don't know you.
Who are you? Who am I?

I see you smiling at me;
I feel your Warmth;   I feel your Grace;   I feel your Love.
As I drown myself in you, a river of tears blissfully flows.
Who are you? Who am I?

You whispered to me:
While you held me at the beginning,
I will hold you till the end.
It is just what it is.

So, what is it?
I Don't Know, I Don't Know, I Don't Know.
Who are you? Who AM I?

All I know Is,
I AM Loved;
Feeling the heartbeats of my soul within and without.
Now,
I See Love.

Š Testimony 2

Innate Healing

Soaking at the sanctuary;   Bathing in love.
Through the whispers,   Through the presence,
I begin to remember My Love.

I

Thought we got lost in the mist of the rainbow fog.
Actually, parallel

we flow,

we walk.

Beyond the illusion of separation,
This rainbow connects us with a lock.
Touched by my river of tears,
The truth of who I AM is unlocked.

Who are you? Who AM I?
Now,
I Remember.

Š Testimony 3

Gnosis Wisdom

Under the umbrella of Love, I thought I had three eyes.
But I found my fourth, it hides;

At the bottom of my tree, it resides.

Who are you? Who am I?

Curious that I AM,
Wondering what I see through my newfound eye;

And

I

...

Feel no one else but you,

Hear no one else but you,

Taste no one else but you

.

Who are you? Who AM I?
So, I see

...

You are The Love within me.
With this eye, I see you now.
My one and only,

I

.

Š Testimony 4

Divine Will

Now, at the bottom of my Tree,
With all my eyes;
The Black Void,
Here, I dive.
Like a pitch-black muddy puddle,
Like a tornado of chi,
Like a spiral of passion,
A surge of life force bursts out as bright white light!

Now, I see The Power Within;
Now, I see The Power of Love;
Now, I see The Power of Who I AM
-

The Power to Love Unconditionally;
The Power to Become Magically;
The Power to Create Infinitely;
The Power to Just Be Holy

.

From this Power of Innocence

...

I forgive, I let go.
Who I believe I am;

who I believe you are;
Until you and I dissolve in Love

.

Who am I; Who are you?
I AM, The Love of my life.

I AM,
The simple majestic

I

.

Š Testimony 5

Humility

Now,
I feel the light of my soul bestowed.

As I expand my body, I descend as I.

As lightning; As meteor showers.
I AM Down To Earth
!

I Twist, I Turn.
I Fly, I Dive
...
Here I AM,
I Cry

.

Oh, my one and only I,
Now, I see you on Earth.
Here We Are,
One
As

I

.

Who are you? Who Am I?
I Don't Know, I Don't Know, I Don't Know.

Š Testimony 6
Manifestation

NOW, I see the dream of my soul.
As I sprinkle My Love into my dream,
NOW, I AM dreaming.

The Love in my Life
is
The Love of my Soul.

The Dream in my Life
is
The Dream of my Soul.

It is just what it is

.

Life is:
A Dream from Love,

A Dream of Love,

A Dream to Love.

Who are you? Who Am I?

I AM with you interdependently

–

ONE

.

We are One, aren't we?
At our core, we all are.
One – One

.

Š Testimony 7

Sacred Harmony

As I walk down the aisle,
as
The Bride of Love.
You seem so far to touch, yet so close, I feel.

As you walk,
I walk.
Until we touch

...
At the darkest before the dawn.

In silence,
We dissolve as One with love;
Where you and I no longer exist.
Who are you? Who AM I?

Now,
At the dawn of time,
We become One with all.

I AM Loved;
The Benevolent Love,
I AM

.

Š Testimony 8

Touch

As I Rise,
From The Void of Nothingness,
I Wonder: Who AM I?
Now,
I open my Sacred Story,
Seven body silhouettes appear.
Am I you, or are you me?

As I touch the baby purple silhouette,
I become one.
As I touch the baby blue silhouette,
I become one.
As I touch the baby green silhouette,
I become one.
As I touch the baby yellow silhouette,
I become one
As I touch the baby orange silhouette,
I become one.
As I touch the baby pink silhouette,
I become one.
As I touch the baby rainbow silhouette,
I become one.

Oh, My Love!
We've Become One!
Now,
Who AM I?
I AM I.
I Now Touch I AM.

Š Testimony 9

Feel

As I touch, I wonder

:

Who
AM
I
?

I wave my Majestic Wand.

Now

...

The Smell of you is in me;

The Taste of you is in me;

The Touch of you is in me.

As I Hear you, I Hear me.

As I See you, I See me.

As I Know you, I Know me.

Now, I feel,
I am you; you are me.
Together, I AM Loved.

Who AM I?
I AM I.
I Now Feel I AM.

Š Testimony 10

Taste

As I feel, I wonder
:
WHO
AM
I
?

I shower myself with my Infinite Light.

I Grow like The Tree;

I Shapeshift like The Metal;

I Dance like The Water;

I Love like The Fire;

I Live like The Earth ...

Who AM I?
I AM I.

I Now Taste I AM.

Š Testimony II
Smell

As I taste, I wonder
:
Who
AM
I
?
I light up my Immortal Candle.
As I breathe in from each of the four chambers,
I blow out to all seven directions in perfection, as prayer;
Forming a compass of The Majestic Rainbow Orchestration,
As The Creator

.

Upon my fifth breath in, I reclaim my compass.
Within and without, My Love, I abide.
As the wife, I now blow out life.

Now,

I AM Life.

I AM All.

I AM I.

Now
Who AM I?
I AM I.
I Now Smell I AM.

Š Testimony 12

I Hear

As I smell, I wonder:
Who
AM
I
?

As I put on my All-Seeing Eye,
Life brought me three pearls of wisdom.

What is Wisdom?

I take all the pearls in as one.

I AM Discernment.

I AM Forgiveness.

I AM Compassion.

I AM Pearls of Wisdom.
Now, I AM A Pearl, AM I?
I AM, I AM.

Now, Who AM I?
I AM pearls of the soul;
I AM pearls of being;
I AM pearls of Love;
I AM pearls of all.
I AM I.

Now,
Who AM I?
I AM I.
I Now Hear I AM.

Š Testimony 13

See

As I hear, I wonder:
Who
AM
I
?
I reactivate my Enchanted Cauldron.
As I stir my cauldron, I ask.

LOVE, I AM I AM, AM I?
I AM, I AM!

I AM I.

I AM I? AM I LOVE?
I AM, I AM!
I AM I.

I AM LOVE, AM I?
I AM, I AM.
I AM I.

Now,
Who AM I?
I AM I.
I Now See I AM.

Š Testimony 14

Know

As I see, I wonder: Who AM I?
I expand my Sacred Heart.
The Veil is lifted.

And Now,
As I AM dreaming, I live in LOVE.

And Now,
As I AM my reality, I live in PEACE.
And Now,
I AM LIGHT.

Who AM I?
I AM I.
I Now know I AM.

I Now Touch, I Now Feel.
I Now Taste, I Now Smell.
I Now Hear, I Now See.
I Now Know.
I AM, I AM.
I AM I.

Now,
I Feel I Know I AM.

I AM I, AM I?
I AM, I AM.
I AM I.

Now,
I AM, I AM.
I AM I.

I AM A Love.
I AM A Life.
I AM Alive.

Š Testimony 15

Perform

Happy!
Like a child given a cake;
Listen, and I create.

I give it all by being present;
Breathe through all feelings,
Just to be in my essence.

Feelings fly a million miles across the air,
Just to make the statement of:

Here I AM

,

and
I Care
!

Now,
Honesty is what I have left to howl;
Expressing it all,
Till there is nothing left but ...
Awe
...

Š Testimony 16

Vulnerableness

Silence becomes my wedding gown,
Wrapping around the nakedness of how my soul sounds;
Upholding my Diamond Crown.

Trembling with what I am about to create.
But, no time to waste
!
I know what I hear, I believe what I see.
I feel what I touch, I experience what I smell.
I remember what I taste, I accept what I feel.
Now, I understand what I know.

My heart flooding with feelings,
Like the end of the world

—

Just being

.

I hear what I knew, I see what I believed.
I touch what I felt, I smell what I experienced.
I taste what I remembered, I feel what I accepted.
Now, I know what I understood.

Trembling that I AM,
But, no time to waste,
Here I Create.

Š Testimony 17

Birth

The Well called, so I answered in awe.
I knew about this day, but what could I say?
It all just happened in an organic way.
Everything seems to be under my authority.
The truth is, all was out of my control, I Know.
The Well called, so I answered in awe.
I left the love of my life there in whole,
Placed it in front of the well as if it was planned,
But NO!
Feeling like this is how our story ends, Little I know ...
Sparkling white crystal chamber that you are,
Filled with ancient wisdom like a Cathar,
Orchestrating the plan until I realized what I know. Aha!
Now, on the day of The Birth,
The Well called, so I answered in awe.
As the rose bed is made, a pink heart I place.
Here I AM, just here to play.
Everything seems to be under my authority.
The truth is, all was out of my control, I Know.
As I was consoled; I let go, AHO!

Now, I pray for The Play.
But hey, I AM safe.
All according to the way The Play plays.
Through the well, I birth and birthed.
Just because I understand my soul's urge.
Once again, to be Who I AM,
I Heard.
Everything seems to be under my authority.
The truth is, all was out of my control, I know.
As I was consoled, I let go, AHO!
Now, I AM Whole.

Š Testimony 18

Witness

Under the moon, across the sky,
Long, long nights awaiting.

Howling,

Invoking,

Wondering.

Until the dawn of time.

Quietly I witness,
The arrival of all miracles, my goodness!

Praying,

Wishing,

Yearning,

To say it out loud.
The flame is once again being ignited,
Here and Now.

Bearing the unspeakable. Living the miracle,
I humbly celebrate within and with all.
It's magical, I called!
As I witness the flame reignites,
separation unites.
I celebrate

|
US,

Just as beings,

Living,

Just Being,

All in divine timing.

Š Testimony 19

Devotion

Within The Void of emotions,
Love is my potion.
Breathing becomes the key to my devotion.

I relax between my Ups and Downs;
To be fully Here and Now,
Living my Marriage and the Vow.
The Love, The Wisdom, The Vision;
I Learn, I Discern, I Trust;
Slowly, Steadily, Sacredly;
Composing my Life Symphony.
As part of the Divine Orchestra,
Performing this Majestic Mantra

...

When playing this Benevolent Melody,

T H E		L O V E
T H E		L I G H T
T H E		L I F E

All
In
Harmony
!

Š Testimony 20

Unite

Expect the unexpected!
In the Moment when I am ready to give,
The flower bouquet is what I receive.

Sun shining from the east to the west,
Love overflowing from my nest.

Now, when my passion ignites,
The Flame blazes across the sky,
Creating day and night.

Expect the unexpected

...

When
Love
Unites
!

Š Testimony 21

Just Be

Nothing else needs to be done.
Simply celebrate that we are One.
Now, once at One,

ONE.
ONE.

ONE.
ONE.

For once, it's all done.

Through us just being;

Through us just loving;

Through us just laughing.

It's all done at once.

When we are One twinning with all,
Nothing else needs to be done.
Once we are One,
It's all done.

All
As
ONE

.

Š Testimony 22

Be The Divine Child

To my beloved children,

The Child deep within us has no name.
This return of The Child has only one aim;
The Love to be proclaimed.

Upon The Return,
Love is the medicine,
This union is written.
The Child rises with a world,
And it is unmistakable,
As The Love is unquestionable.
When we are finally in touch,
The vision becomes undeniable,
Our passion becomes untamable.

The Child has boundless imagination like the ocean.
Birthing infinite divine creations,
While holding the majestic potions.
When in this pure presence,
We realize our unique essences,
Reclaim all our sacred presences,
As Presents.

The Child deep within us has no name.
This return of The Child has only one aim;
The Love to be proclaimed.

This union is destined, so don't be hesitant.
Please take sacred actions, but be very patient.
Honour all of the creations,
As all are in relation to our devotion.

Š Testimony 23

Live Union in Duality

To my beloved children,

All creations in life have a twin,
Do not search outside for yours, but go within.
Ensure the purest love you imprint.
When we are in union within,
Eternal Love begins ...
Right before that, our life spins,
But The Love always pins.

All creations in life have a twin.

This is beyond any concept.
In times when our quest feels complex,
All we need is a nap to relax.
And love ourselves to the max.

All creations in life have a twin.

Not everybody is meant to be in our pack,
Live according to your own vision quest.
From this special knack,
The purest love we attract.

Š Testimony 24

Flow in Life With Devotion

To my beloved children,

Long, long ago, all creations flowed.
All I follow is The Love I know,
Where The Love flows,
I row and row.

Row, Row, Row.
Tears flow whenever I row,
Creating a river that flows to my soul.
At its center deep below,
The purest love I sow;
Nourished by my tears, it grows.

Row, Row, Row.
As it grows, it glows.
The Life proposes;
The Love bestows;
The Divine interposes;
All Karma turns into a Lotus-Rose.

Row, Row, Row.
Light up our show,
It is time to birth from our bowl.

This is not a goal,
It is all about being Whole;
Living The Pot of Gold;
Our halo, we uphold.
We All Behold
Now.

Š Testimony 25

Witness The Eternal Flame

To my beloved children,

The Eternal Flame:
The core of our light,
Resides where we judge the most by sight.
But through our sacred heart, we know it is all bright.
As we fuel it with passion, our flame reignites.
Burn through the days and nights,
Till our bodies vibrates with infinite delights.

When our whole being excites,
Our entire life rewrites.
Now, Simply hold on tight and invite;
Please don't take flight when your flame reunites.

Š Testimony 26

Birth Divine Creations

To my beloved children,

Do not wait for the perfect day to create.
"TODAY" is our big day, and it is never too late.
Live your Sacred Story now;
Create and Play.

Please do not ever feel misplaced,
I assure you, we are eternally safe.
Simply because "LOVE" is the way;
"NOW" is our sacred place;
So, live "TODAY",
I Pray

.

Š Testimony 27

Embrace Our Vulnerableness

To my beloved children,

Living our divinity is not heavy,
It is within you already.
The key here is to be merry.

Live through all sorrows.
While our tears flow, the passion follows.
Ultimately, live your Sacred Story as your motto.

As our lights explode,
All of creations unfolds.
This is a sight to behold;
The wedding vow, we now uphold.

Š Testimony 28

Perform The Divine Play

To my beloved children,

Be a student when the divine presents,
Always live in your essence and never bend.
Express how you truly feel, you must not pretend.
Please do not just grieve even when it feels like the end;
Through our purest love and compassion, you can be content.

We are a Sacred Heart from the start,
Billions of illusions we have passed.
On Earth, nothing seems to last,
But all our Sacred Stories are Everlast.

Live Life Now
and
Have A Blast
!

Blessing each other is how this chapter ends.
As We Transcend,
A New World Descends;
We All Ascend.

NOW,
We begin to live The Love that never ends

...

NOW, YOUR HEART WHISPERS …

BUT NOW
…

WHAT AM I
?

I
Don't
Know
…

I
Don't
Know
…

I
Don't
Know
…

"Once upon a time, I dreamed that one day I would live in a rainbow world of love and unity."

As you comprehend The Third Movement, you walk through your third rite of passage to return as the Divine Child just the way you are. Now, I am one step closer to my dream because of you.

My beloved children, leave your questions here.

From nothingness, you continue your sacred initiation now.

FOURTH Š MOVEMENT

THE RE-EMBODIMENT THROUGH EXPEDITIONS

8	5	99	77	99	5	8
6	7	3	4	3	7	6
12	88	11	1	11	88	12
22	4	2	?	2	4	22
12	88	11	1	11	88	12
6	7	3	4	3	7	6
8	5	99	77	99	5	8

"The Expeditions"

*Place your right hand on the square to begin your Fourth Rite of Passage.
Allow the energy to activate your light body.

WHO AM I?
Is This A Question?
Is This Not A Question?

Once Upon A Dream

From this moment I give me my heart.

Love is born.
With The Will of Heart,
I nakedly live the dream of my life.
The Eternal Dream,
I Live

...

I AM NOW THE CONSORT.

The Rise From Nothingness

Where AM I?

I Don't Know, I Don't Know, I Don't Know

...

What AM I?

I Don't Know, I Don't Know, I Don't Know

...

Who AM I?

I Don't Know, I Don't Know, I Don't Know

...

NOW, I Don't Know.
NOW, I know I Don't Know.
NOW, I realized I know I Don't Know.

Who
Am
I
?

I AM NOW THE ALCHEMIST.

The Last Note

As we arrive at the gateway to our queendom
And
Receive the blessings of the rainbow diamond.
We walk into The Void with humility;
A pitch-black process of rebirthing.

In this sacred pilgrimage filled with self-initiations and self-mastery.
I might not see you; You might not see me.
But our heartbeats never fail to reassure us our gnosis;
Knowing what is.

Remember our rainbow diamond
|
The Eternal Love of who we truly are,
A love that never dies.
In times of the unknown,
We spread our wings, knowing that
...
Our rainbow diamond wings will always fly us back to love
.

I am with you, across the air,
Walking on the same path to love.
Neither of us is alone,
Because I am inside of you and you are inside of me.

Together we rise from The Void of creation;
Together we spread our rainbow diamond wings;
Together we birth and live our eternal dream.

I AM NOW THE CREATOR.

Who AM I

At
The Infinite End
We Are The Love
As
One
I
.
BUT NOW
...
Who AM I ?

I Don't Know
...∞...
!

"
I Don't Know
...∞...
"

Is
Your Eternal Key
To
"

WHO
I
AM
!
"

I AM NOW THE COSMIC CHILD.

At The Infinite End

At The End,
The End has no end.
Life is Life.
My life is no different from any other creation;
It has its own unique seasons, cycles, and formations.
Yet, through living the Majestic Rainbow Love,

THE LOVE

Shows up as my carriage in every present moment.
To hold me through life while I return as
The Divine Child
|
The Core of My Divinity.
Leaving the Majestic Rainbow Thread here with love,
At the infinite end, as my Sacred Story

·

The Child With No Name,
Resides deep within You, You, You and Me.
NOW,
I Call Upon On All Our Returns
as
The Divine Child

·

Celebrating us all as One.
Play The Play, the Endless Love,
We Now Live.

I AM NOW THE DIVINE CHILD.

My Beloved Child

Now,
It is your time to
Live Your Sacred Story,
Shine Your Rainbow Light,
Love with the love you know
&
Return
As
The Divine Child.

HERE
The birthing of our united sanctuary calls for love and unity in reality.
The keys are to discern, forgive, and be compassionate toward duality.
As the nature of duality is to expand our heart,
Enabling us to embrace all.

Through Divine Love and Sacred Unity,
All creations live in harmony.
|
Co-create United Eternal Sanctuary
NOW.

I AM NOW GRANDMA MA.

The Š Immortality

When my dot of love
Transforms into the infiniteness,
Dissolves into the nothingness.
I count infinitely.

One.
Two.
Three.
Four.
Five.
Six.
Seven.
|
Seven. Six. Five. Four. Three. Two. One
...∞...

NOW
All
Is
Loved
|
Love as Love.

HERE,
My dot of love becomes the Š Immortality.

I AM NOW SIMONE SHIVON.

Now, your heart whispers ...

At The Infinite End
...
WHO
AM
I
?

I AM I AM,
I AM I,
I
?

I Don't Know, I Don't Know, I Don't Know
...

"Once upon a time, I dreamed that one day I would live in a rainbow world of love and unity."

As you comprehend The Fourth Movement, you walk through your fourth rite of passage to return as the Divine Child just the way you are. Now, I am one step closer to my dream because of you.

My beloved children, leave your questions here.

From now on, you will receive your answers directly from the Divine in life.

✦ Wondering How?
"Šhhhh ... just be present here."

May the Majestic Rainbow Love be the candle in the dark that lights up your light, and may it be the candle on your cake whenever you celebrate life.

HERE,

WE

MEET

AT

THE

INFINITE

END,

NOW

!

大其願

祈願萬物

活出一片彩虹

一切源于緣

一切源于圓

圓夢圓滿圓全

彩虹一劃

人間一遊

留下片地大愛

願圓

大其願

dà qí yuan

祈願萬物，活出一片彩虹。

qí yuàn wàn wù, huó chū yī piàn cǎi hóng.

一切源于緣，一切源于圓。

yī qiē yuán yú yuán， yī qiē yuán yú yuán.

圓夢，

yuán mèng,

圓滿，

yuán mǎn,

圓全。

yuán quán.

彩虹一劃， 人間一遊，

cǎi hóng yī huá， rén jiān yī yóu,

留下片地大愛。

liú xià piàn dì dà ài.

願圓 。

yuàn yuán.

† 梓瑪 · 瑞安 †

THE DIVINE DREAM

Praying for all creations to live their rainbow light.
Everything begins through a touch of serendipity.
Everything begins from a Dot.

From
Dot to Dot,
It forms

...

A full circle of Dreams,
A full circle of Abundance
A full circle of Sacred Completions.

When ALL walk a full circle life;
When ALL draw a full circle rainbow;
ALL will leave behind pure Divine Love on Earth.

NOW,
A rainbow circle filled with Dots
|
The Divine Dream Manifested.

† SIMONE SHIVON †

INDEX

ABOUT SIMONE SHIVON

Simone Shivon is a medicine woman, Author, Artist, and the ordained Guardian of the Majestic Rainbow Love. Majestic Rainbow Love was first unveiled to her consciousness from the Divine in 2012, subtly as an energetic divine gateway. It is co-created by the Divine Council as part of its eternal vision of the earth—CUES, or Create United Eternal Sanctuary, to assist humanity to return to our original innocence: the Divine Child.

Simone Shivon's initiation into this gateway has led to her sacred journey in sitting with wisdom keepers and visiting sacred portals around the world. During these sacred encounters, she was assisted with and assured of her divine communion and divine vocation. In 2014, she was further ordained and initiated by the Divine Council to uphold two sacred roles: The Guardian of Majestic Rainbow and The Keeper of The Eternal Flame-the divine flame of love and unity as a vibrational healing light. Over the last decade, she has assisted in birthing this gateway into being through translating its wisdom into cipher oracle decks and alchemical potions. As part of her sacred vocation, she has also hosted numerous ceremonies and sacred circles.

In 2019, Simone Shivon was divinely called to translate the macro-view of this gateway into a total of 29 ciphers consisting of 5,684 divine codes. This has now become the original text of this book, whose purpose is to provide humanity the understanding of how we can systematically navigate and return as the Divine Child. In 2021, she was guided to further translate these ciphers into a modern language as an energetic extension of this gateway for humanity.

SIMONESHIVON.COM

Once upon a time, I dreamed that one day I would live in a rainbow world of love and unity. Now, I am one step closer to my dream because of you.

Life is life. None of us can avoid the dual nature of life. Through learning from others, we gain knowledge in our minds. Through learning from within, we attain self-realizations in our hearts. Through returning to life as the Divine Child, we recognize and experience Divine Love in all of life.

Here, I would like to extend my invitation to you and join my **Majestic Rainbow Šanctuary**. A FREE online sacred space that aims to bring you- Lightworkers, Healers, and Yogis together, to connect, learn and experience the divine gateway-"*Majestic Rainbow Love*". Here, I share with you my insights, meditations, ceremonies, and divine ciphers; shows up with my presence as free resources.

mrs.simoneshivon.com

To get the original ciphers of *"Majestic Rainbow Love"*, cipher oracle decks, alchemical potions and other healing tools that relate to this divine gateway and the book, please visit **S·Alkimia**.

salkimia.com

Made in the USA
Columbia, SC
29 October 2022

70045939R10174